# thriving
## as a
# new
## teacher

tools and strategies for your first year

# JOHN F. ELLER & SHEILA A. ELLER

Solution Tree | Press

a division of
Solution Tree

555 North Morton Street
Bloomington, IN 47404
800.733.6786 (toll free) / 812.336.7700
FAX: 812.336.7790

email: info@solution-tree.com
solution-tree.com

Visit **go.solution-tree.com/instruction** to download the free reproducibles in this book.

Printed in the United States of America

20  19  18  17  16                          1  2  3  4  5

Library of Congress Control Number: 2016930937

**Solution Tree**
Jeffrey C. Jones, CEO
Edmund M. Ackerman, President

**Solution Tree Press**
*President*: Douglas M. Rife
*Senior Acquisitions Editor*: Amy Rubenstein
*Editorial Director*: Lesley Bolton
*Managing Production Editor*: Caroline Weiss
*Senior Production Editor*: Suzanne Kraszewski
*Copy Editor*: Ashante K. Thomas
*Proofreader*: Elisabeth Abrams
*Cover and Text Designer*: Laura Kagemann

# Acknowledgments

Solution Tree Press would like to thank the following reviewers:

Julie Bonfield
Curriculum Specialist
Montgomery County Public Schools
Mount Sterling, Kentucky

Tracey Garrett
Associate Professor, Department of Teacher Education
Rider University
Lawrenceville, New Jersey

Rebecca A. Krystyniak
Director, Teacher Preparation Initiative
Professor, Department of Chemistry and Physics
St. Cloud State University
St. Cloud, Minnesota

Lauren Morgan
Grade Two Teacher
Franklin Sherman Elementary School
McLean, Virginia

Chris Porter
Instructional Specialist
Katy Independent School District
Katy, Texas

Visit **go.solution-tree.com/instruction**
to access free materials related to this book.

# Table of Contents

# About the Authors

**John F. Eller, PhD,** has served as director of the educational leadership doctoral program at St. Cloud State University, worked with educational leaders at Virginia Polytechnic Institute and State University, and developed teacher leaders in a master's program. He is a former principal, director of a principal's training center, and assistant superintendent for curriculum, learning, and staff development. He has served as executive director of the Minnesota State affiliate of ASCD (formerly the Association for Supervision and Curriculum Development).

John specializes in implementing effective teaching strategies; dealing with difficult people; building professional learning communities; conducting employee evaluations; building conferencing and coaching skills; developing strategic planning strategies; planning and implementing school-improvement initiatives; using differentiated instruction; leading, selecting, and inducting employees; and building supervisory skills. He has authored *Effective Group Facilitation in Education: How to Energize Meetings and Manage Difficult Groups*, and coauthored *Working With and Evaluating Difficult School Employees, So Now You're the Superintendent!, Energizing Staff Meetings,* and *Creative Strategies to Transform School Culture.* He is also coauthor of *Working With Difficult and Resistant Staff* and *Score to Soar: Moving Teachers From Evaluation to Professional Growth.*

John earned a doctorate in educational leadership and policy studies from Loyola University Chicago and a master's degree in educational leadership from the University of Nebraska Omaha.

**Sheila A. Eller, EdD,** is a middle school principal for Mounds View Public Schools in Minnesota. She has served as a principal in Fairfax County (Virginia) Public Schools and other schools in Minnesota. Sheila is a former principal, university professor, special education teacher, Title I mathematics teacher, and self-contained classroom teacher for grades 1–4.

In Fairfax County, Sheila helped transform a school that was not making adequate yearly progress, served a low socioeconomic–status population, and had a high minority population through professional learning community implementation, data use, and refinement of teaching and learning strategies.

Sheila shares her expertise at international conferences and with school districts in the areas of school turnaround, effective instruction, teacher evaluation, building leadership teams, teacher leadership, and various other topics. As a professor at National Louis University in Chicago, she worked on the development team for a classroom mathematics series, and her teaching skills were featured on a video that accompanied the series. She has coauthored *Energizing Staff Meetings*, *Working With and Evaluating Difficult School Employees*, and *Creative Strategies to Transform School Culture*. She is also coauthor of *Working With Difficult and Resistant Staff* and *Score to Soar: Moving Teachers from Evaluation to Professional Growth*.

She has been a member of the Minnesota ASCD executive board and a regional president of the Minnesota Elementary School Principals' Association.

Sheila received a doctorate in educational leadership and administration from St. Cloud State University, a master's degree from Creighton University, and a bachelor's degree from Iowa State University.

To learn more about John and Sheila's work, visit www.ellerandassociates .com or follow them on Twitter @jellerthree.

To book John Eller or Sheila Eller for professional development, contact pd@solution-tree.com.

# Preparing for the First Year

*It is August, and Karla, a new high school English teacher, is working to get her classroom ready for the first day of class. As she works, her mind races with thoughts of all that lies ahead: What will her students be like? How can she build relationships with them? Will she be able to engage her students in the content? How will she deal with disruptive student behavior and parental concerns, meet her principal's expectations, manage the curriculum, and accurately assess her students? There is so much Karla needs to think about for her first teaching job. She feels overwhelmed.*

Karla's feelings as she approaches the start of school are common among teachers entering the profession. Teaching is a highly rewarding career, but it is a difficult one as well—one that has both rewards and challenges. Welcome to teaching!

Teaching is like a vocation because it is more than just a job; it is a lifelong endeavor for most people who enter the profession. Great teachers enter the profession because they want to make a difference in the lives of their students. It takes passion and lots of dedication to do well as a teacher. Some teachers seem to be cut out to be teachers from an early age while others find their passion and come into teaching later in their lives. When someone decides to become a teacher, he or she should know that though the profession involves many rewards, it also has many challenges. As a teacher, you are going to change lives. Historian Henry Brooks Adams said, "A teacher affects eternity: he can never tell where his influence stops." Indeed, a good teacher's influence can never be erased.

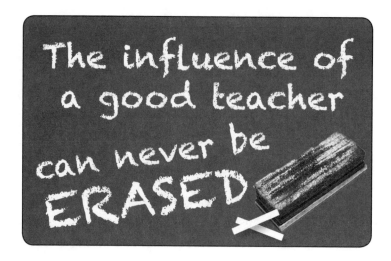

The influence of a good teacher can never be ERASED

## Your First Teaching Job

Congratulations! You have made a successful transition from student to teacher. This transition likely seems daunting. You will encounter many challenges during your career. Some challenges will seem minor, while others will test you to the limit.

Your first experience as a teacher is crucial to your future success in the profession. This first experience will shape your perception of teaching and help you decide if it is the right career for you.

## A Thriving New Teacher

Throughout this book, we use the term *thriving new teacher* to describe teachers who are reaching an optimal performance level. A thriving new teacher is someone who has comfortably moved into the profession by overcoming the initial challenges he or she encountered in order to become proficient in the skills and techniques needed to be effective in working with students. A thriving new teacher has pushed beyond feeling nervous and overwhelmed to feeling confident and effective. This new teacher understands that there is still room for improvement and that he or she has overcome some of the initial issues and challenges that can get in the way of success.

Thriving new teachers focus on several critical areas related to their teaching. These are the areas that impact them and their students the most, from knowledge and care of themselves as teachers to understanding and implementing effective assessments to working effectively with colleagues.

## The Six Spheres

The areas that help new teachers thrive are represented by the six spheres. These six spheres (shown in figure I.1) provide the foundation for this book.

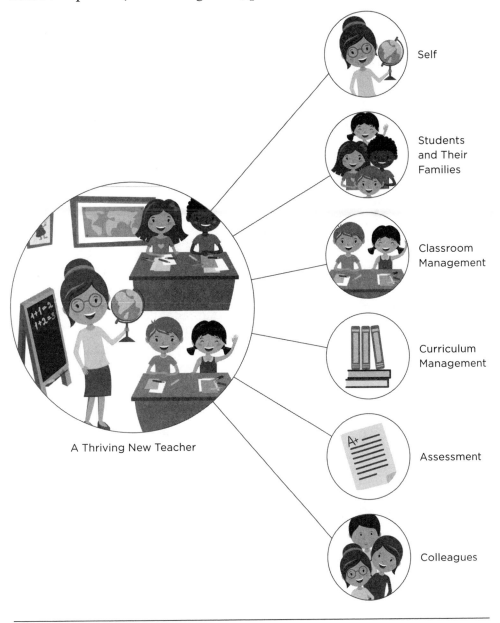

Figure I.1: Six spheres of focus for thriving new teachers.

In this book, we provide skills and strategies to support each sphere. A brief description of each sphere follows.

- **Self:** Thriving new teachers have a positive attitude and good self-esteem, and are able to build rapport with others. They possess good communication skills.

- **Students and their families:** Thriving new teachers believe that students, along with their families, can be successful and are interested in learning and growing. These teachers build on student strengths and help them experience success and involve their families as partners.

- **Classroom management:** Thriving new teachers structure their classroom procedures for success so that students can learn in a safe environment. These teachers operate their classrooms in a consistent and fair manner. They know how to prevent disruptions, but if they occur, they know how to quickly deescalate them.

- **Curriculum management:** Thriving new teachers make content learnable, interesting, and relevant to their students. They know how to pace the content so students can learn. They also understand the importance of the right learning targets and learner-appropriate methods to maximize student growth and achievement.

- **Assessment:** Thriving new teachers design effective assessments to measure their teaching effectiveness and their students' growth. They use these assessments to make instructional decisions for future learning targets and teaching methods for their students. The assessment strategies they implement include regular, formative methods coupled with culminating, summative methods.

- **Colleagues:** Thriving new teachers understand the importance of collegial relationships, learning from their peers, and supporting them as interdependent team members. These teachers also understand and follow school policies and procedures. In addition, they have a clear focus on ethical professional practices and engage in professional development to maintain and refine their teaching skills and strategies.

In the chapters that follow, you will find information, strategies, and tools to develop your essential skills in these six spheres to become a thriving new teacher.

## How This Book Is Organized

This book is organized into chapters that incorporate the six spheres model outlined in the previous section. In chapter 1, you will examine yourself and the gifts you bring to teaching. This information will help provide the "rudder" that will guide you on your journey to becoming a thriving new teacher. In chapter 2, we examine the importance of your first days as a teacher and making a positive and lasting impression with students and families as well as colleagues. Chapter 3 outlines the importance of moving beyond the initial impression and developing long-term relationships with students. Chapters 4 and 5 discuss the important topics of classroom management and working successfully with difficult students. These chapters provide the foundations for success as a new teacher. Chapter 6 outlines information about managing the curriculum and your course content. Chapter 7 deals with formative and summative assessment, and chapter 8 provides you with a multitude of strategies designed to help make learning active and keep students engaged and interested in learning. All of the chapters work together to help you thrive as a new teacher.

# chapter 1

# Understanding Yourself

*Antonio, a new high school history teacher, has just completed his first quarter at Armstrong High School. The start of the school year was hectic, and Antonio feels like he has been on a treadmill— moving all the time just to stay on track. While some of the teaching strategies he has tried have worked well, others have not been so successful. At the end of each day, Antonio takes time to reflect on his teaching and the challenges he has faced. During this reflection time, it's easy for a new teacher to be more critical than positive about his or her teaching.*

*Luckily for Antonio, at the beginning of the school year he spent some time thinking about his strengths and limitations, and he set some reasonable goals for himself as a teacher. In addition to regularly reviewing and adjusting his goals, Antonio meets often with his mentor teacher. In their conversations, Antonio and his mentor discuss both the challenges he faces and the positive progress he has made as a new teacher. These balanced conversations help Antonio and his mentor view Antonio's teaching realistically so they can determine how he can continue to improve.*

Antonio experienced the normal phases that new teachers go through in their first job. Earlier in the fall, he moved from anxiously anticipating the start of the school year, to feeling overwhelmed, to finally questioning himself and his abilities as a teacher. Many new teachers go through the same phases during their initial experiences. Antonio had anticipated these phases and spent time thinking about them and identifying his strengths and limitations so he could call on them when he needed them. The foundation of self-understanding that Antonio developed helped him stay on course while others can get stuck in the phases. Some new teachers are able to emerge with confidence while others may begin to question their effectiveness and commitment to teaching.

As a thriving new teacher, you should focus first on yourself—your personality, skills, and what you bring to the position. Your background and experiences, your strengths, your limitations, and your personality are all important factors in your success. In this chapter, we examine several ways to help you understand yourself and some of the changes you may go through as you experience your first year as a new teacher.

In spite of all the exciting materials, interesting content, and new technologies available to teachers, the one aspect that makes the most difference in the success of students is the teacher him- or herself. If you have a sound understanding of yourself as a teacher, you can use all the various tools, techniques, and strategies available to you to make a difference in the lives of your students.

You may feel like you are riding a roller coaster your first year teaching. At times, you will feel a sense of excitement, while at other times you'll wonder why you even wanted to be a teacher in the first place. It's important to understand that going through different emotional phases as a new teacher is perfectly normal. The New Teacher Center at the University of California, Santa Cruz, identifies a model that we find helpful to new teachers (Moir, 2011). This information appears in the self section because the new teacher phases impact how you perceive your effectiveness as a thriving new teacher.

Figure 1.1 summarizes the phases in the new teacher phase model.

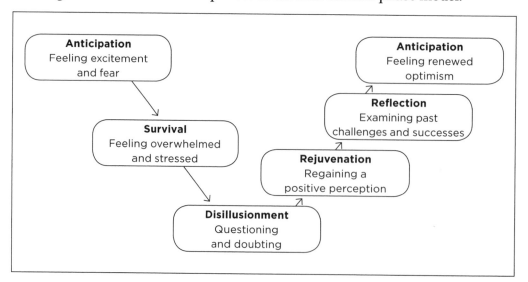

Source: Adapted from Moir, 2011.

Figure 1.1: Phases of first-year teachers' attitudes toward teaching.

## The Phases and Their Impact on You as a New Teacher

Many new teachers find their first year to be their most challenging. Though excited for the opportunity to work with students, new educators often realize that being an effective teacher entails more than creating and teaching lesson plans. According to Ellen Moir (2011), founder and chief executive officer of the New Teacher Center, there are six emotional phases of first-year teaching: anticipation, survival, disillusionment, rejuvenation, reflection, and then anticipation again. The following details each of these phases and includes recommendations for successfully navigating them.

### Anticipation

In the anticipation phase, you may feel excited about the impact you can make on your students. This phase can start during your student-teaching experience and continue through the first few weeks of school. In the anticipation phase, you may feel excited and scared at the same time.

While not everyone has the same emotions in this phase, there are several strategies that new teachers may find helpful to stay centered. The following strategies will help you as you work through the anticipation phase.

▸ Understand that the feelings you are experiencing are real and normal.

▸ Write down some of your feelings and goals in a journal that you keep throughout your first year.

▸ In many schools, new teachers are assigned mentors, coaches, and other peers who work with them and help them make a successful transition into the classroom. If you have such a support person, schedule an appointment with your mentor to discuss your goals.

Let's see how Antonio, the thriving new teacher in our example at the beginning of the chapter, used these strategies as he encountered the anticipation phase.

> As he was preparing his classroom during the fall workshop days, Antonio started to become excited when he thought about the upcoming year. What would the students be like? How would they react to his ideas and strategies? How would he do as a new teacher? Antonio's mentor, Hermine, had scheduled a meeting with him to discuss the upcoming year. Antonio decided to use this initial meeting to help him explore his foundations as a teacher. Since the first time he met Hermine, he trusted her and knew she was the sort of mentor who could help him as he began his teaching career.

*Antonio completed a self-assessment listing some of his strengths and limitations. He also wrote down four goals he had for himself and his students during the first few months of school. During the meeting, Antonio shared his reflections with Hermine. She listened intently and then asked Antonio if he would like some feedback. She then shared her perceptions of his strengths and limitations. She also gave him some perspective on his initial set of goals. Finally, she offered to help him in the areas of planning and assessment since these are the areas Antonio listed as his limitations.*

*After the conversation, Antonio felt good that Hermine was interested in helping him be successful. He felt much calmer in starting the school year.*

In this example, we see how spending a small amount of time before the start of the school year reflecting on teaching and consulting with a supportive mentor can make a big difference as a new teacher. Antonio was able to use the energy normally associated with the anticipation phase to help himself positively focus on real strategies he could employ in his classroom.

## Survival

During the first month of school, you may start to feel overwhelmed. You need to generate several new lessons almost every day, so you find yourself working well beyond the normal school hours and on weekends. Even if you planned over the summer, you soon find that you need to make adjustments, unanticipated issues have arisen, and some of the lessons you planned may not work. As a new teacher, you may find yourself working day to day and even hour by hour in some cases. This can be a stressful time when you feel as though you did not choose the right career and may even contemplate quitting teaching.

The following are some strategies you can use to get through the survival phase.

> ▸ **Understand that the feelings you are experiencing are real and normal.** Some new teachers feel overwhelmed. Others describe that they feel like they are "on a treadmill"—constantly working but not reaching their goals. Still others express a loss of confidence in their teaching and problem-solving skills. If you shrug off or repress these feelings, they may continue in your subconscious to undermine your success.

> ▸ **Talk to your peer coach or mentor.** In this conversation, let him or her know about your feelings and thoughts. Share with your coach or mentor the outcome you are looking for in the conversation. If you are

looking for reassurance, share that at the beginning of the meeting. If you want resources or support, let your mentor or coach know that as well. In many cases, people can't meet our needs unless we let them know what we are looking for.

▶ **Find experienced colleagues who are teaching similar content to yours.** See if they are willing to share ideas and resources that you could use or adapt for your classroom.

▶ **Focus on doing a good job rather than trying to be perfect.** You're still learning; not everything you do will be perfect. Remembering this can help some new teachers decrease the pressure they put on themselves and help to diminish negative thoughts during the survival phase.

▶ **Review the notes you wrote in your journal during the anticipation phase.** Look for the strengths you identified before the start of the school year. Also review what you wrote about why you chose to become a teacher. Reminding yourself of your strengths and aspirations can help you get back on track and provide strength and encouragement.

▶ **Allow yourself opportunities for personal reflection to take stock in your successes as well as your challenges.** As you think about your teaching, focus on the small issues that may be negatively impacting the success of your lesson rather than criticizing yourself and totally scrapping your unsuccessful lessons. Review the expectations you have set for yourself and your teaching. See how you are progressing and take stock in your progress. You may have made more progress than you give yourself credit for.

▶ **Think about the concept of "scope of control" (discussed later in this chapter).** Determine what is within your scope of control and what is outside your scope of control. Focus on how you can impact those factors that are within your scope of control. Think about what you need to do in relation to the factors outside of your scope of control. You can either try to ignore them or you can attempt to increase your influence so you can begin to impact them. Scope of control is a concept that can help all teachers manage situations and issues they may face.

▶ **Build in time for physical exercise, especially during this phase.** Exercise can help you let off a little steam and clear your mind. As you're working, take short breaks to re-energize yourself. Periodic short breaks can actually help you work better than pushing through issues when you're tired or discouraged.

▸ **Find someone (a spouse, family member, friend, or significant other) who is willing to listen to you share both your positive and negative experiences.** This other person may not be able to offer any helpful suggestions, but letting you share your frustrations will help you feel better.

Let's see how Antonio, our thriving new teacher, deals with the pressures of the survival phase.

*At the end of each day, Antonio feels physically and emotionally drained. In addition to teaching all day, he is working late into the evenings and on weekends to plan his lessons. It seems as though no matter how hard he works, he is becoming more and more overwhelmed. Antonio is beginning to second guess his decision to go into teaching.*

*Antonio then remembers what he read about the survival phase for new teachers. He decides to try a few of the strategies he learned to help him manage his emotions during this phase.*

*He decides that he is going to set some limits on the amount of time he works outside of the classroom. He makes a commitment to get thirty minutes of light exercise each day. He also looks at his personal reflections related to why he went into teaching and some of the strengths he possesses as a teacher. In reflecting on his work outside of the classroom, Antonio finds that he was spending a lot of time trying to design perfect lessons. Sometimes, one lesson plan could take him over two hours to develop. As he thinks about it, these "perfect" lessons were not much better than the ones he spent less time planning.*

*By adding exercise, reflecting on his strengths, and focusing on more reasonable expectations, Antonio starts to feel empowered in his situation. Even though he is still very busy, Antonio starts to feel like he is controlling the situation rather than letting the situation control him. This new perspective helps him successfully navigate through the survival phase.*

The survival phase is a difficult phase for most new teachers. Employing some of the strategies presented in this section will help you as you deal with this challenging phase. Since each new teacher and situation is unique, it is important to try a variety of ideas to see which ones work best for you.

## Disillusionment

Disillusionment can typically occur six to eight weeks after a new teacher starts teaching. The feeling of being overwhelmed may be taking its toll. As a new teacher, you work many extra hours just to keep up with the demands of getting lessons ready, managing the classroom, designing assessments, keeping records, and working with parents. On top of that, you may have just finished your first round of parent conferences and been observed for the first time by the principal.

In the disillusionment phase, you might be very hard on yourself, spending a lot of time questioning your competence and commitment to teaching. You are probably beginning to admit that things are not going according to your plan. You may feel that the principal is not happy with your performance or progress and wishes he or she had chosen another candidate. On top of all of this stress, your family members (spouse or significant other, children, parents, and so on) are complaining that you are working all the time, don't seem to have time for them, seem distant, and are lacking patience with them. You may be feeling tired and sick, but you can't take a sick day because your lesson plans are incomplete and work needs to get done.

The following are some strategies to help you get through the disillusionment phase.

▸ Keep in mind that the disillusionment phase is normal and something that most teachers go through at some point. Use this knowledge to identify this phase and how it is impacting you. Awareness can go a long way in helping you move forward.

▸ Talk to your mentor or peer coach. Let him or her know that you believe you are in the disillusionment phase, and ask for help in working your way out of it. Be clear; let your mentor or coach know what you're looking for during your conversations—new ideas, resources, or strategies? If you're looking for someone to just listen and not provide advice, let your mentor know this so he or she doesn't feel obligated to come up with solutions. Being clear about your needs and expectations will help keep the conversation productive.

▸ Focus on your accomplishments. Some new teachers find it helpful to review the journal entries they made before the start of the year related to their strengths and goals. If you choose this strategy, be careful to focus on your achievements, not your limitations. Identify the progress you have made toward your goals rather than focusing on what you have not accomplished. By concentrating on your strengths and accomplishments, you may find yourself feeling less disillusioned and more empowered.

▸ Make sure you are getting plenty of rest and exercise during this time. Even though you are busy, it may help you to take a day during the weekend to recharge. Use this same strategy during holiday breaks. While you may feel compelled to catch up on your work during extended breaks, you will also want to get away from the work for a few days to refresh your thinking.

▸ Use the concept of scope of control to help you identify the aspects of your situation that you can impact and which you can't. Gaining a sense of control can help some new teachers move through the disillusionment phase.

Our thriving new teacher, Antonio, experiences the disillusionment phase. Let's see how he reactes to the situation.

> *After about three months in his new position, Antonio starts to wonder why he became a teacher. While some of his classes are going very well, others are not. He starts thinking that maybe he can't make a difference with students—that he doesn't seem cut out to be a teacher. It is clear Antonio is in the disillusionment phase.*
>
> *When he is faced with these negative thoughts, Antonio remembers what he learned about the disillusionment phase. He schedules a meeting with his mentor, Hermine, to discuss the situation. She listens intently and then reminds Antonio that disillusionment is a common feeling for new teachers. Hermine and Antonio review his journal. She helps Antonio remember that he does have a lot of teaching strengths and that he has made good progress on his teaching goals. She also helps Antonio identify which of his challenges are within his scope of control and in which areas he will have little impact.*
>
> *After their conversation, Antonio feels better. Even though many challenges remain, he feels renewed after working through them with a trusted colleague.*

The disillusionment phase can be very dangerous. It is a time when many new teachers consider leaving the profession. Some people can even get depressed when they feel disillusioned. Being aware of when you have moved into this phase and using some of the strategies presented here will help you get through the phase successfully.

## Rejuvenation

After you make your way out of the disillusionment phase, you may find yourself in a phase called rejuvenation. In this phase, you may experience an increase in your positive perception of teaching. By now, you have been able to recharge during a scheduled school break, you better understand the systems in place at your school, you have a more realistic perception of teaching in general, and you have been able to reflect on and learn from your experiences during the first semester. You may also have had a chance to take some time to lead a more normal lifestyle, get plenty of rest, and more effectively develop lessons and activities that you can implement during the upcoming semester. Your first semester has helped you gain new skills and strategies that you can use to prevent many issues that may have plagued you during the first semester in relation to classroom management, curriculum, planning, and assessment. You have also developed collegial relationships with your mentor and other colleagues. In this phase, you can now begin to focus on moving from day-to-day problem solving to longer-term planning.

Some new teachers find it difficult to overcome the disillusionment phase and get to rejuvenation. Once you have reached rejuvenation, keep the following in mind.

▸ Celebrate the fact that you have survived! Plan to do something special for yourself and enjoy the rejuvenation phase.

▸ Take advantage of your renewed enthusiasm and address some previous issues you faced. You may be able to see these issues with a fresh perspective and develop strategies to help you prevent them in the future.

▸ Talk to your mentor or coach. Celebrate your new enthusiasm and energy together. Ask for ideas and strategies to help you stay in a positive frame of mind for the remainder of the school year. As always, be clear about what you are looking for in a conversation with your mentor or coach.

▸ Take time to continue to recharge. You may face some challenges ahead, so storing energy for future obstacles is important.

Let's revisit our new teacher Antonio and see how he experiences the rejuvenation phase.

> *After several weeks of struggle, Antonio begins to feel more comfortable and confident. The strategies he used while he was feeling disillusioned begin to pay off. He notices that he is starting*

*to become enthusiastic again about his teaching and is feeling like he has more energy to impact some of the issues that are within his scope of control.*

*Since Antonio shared his thoughts with his mentor when he was feeling overwhelmed and disillusioned, he thinks it would be nice to let Hermine know how things are better. He schedules a meeting with her, telling her he wants to share the positive feelings he has been having recently related to his teaching.*

*Hermine comes to Antonio's classroom after school one day prepared to just listen to his positive experiences. As she listens, she can tell that Antonio is in the rejuvenation phase. She encourages him to go back and revisit his journal and his strengths, limitations, and goals to see how he is progressing in these areas. She asks Antonio to talk about how he is feeling and what brought him to his current state of mind. By asking Antonio to discuss this, Hermine is trying to help him see how he worked through the challenging situation. She encourages Antonio to add some notes to his journal about their conversation and congratulates him for moving beyond disillusionment and into this new phase. Antonio is happy he met with Hermine and confident about his teaching going forward.*

Antonio used several strategies for the rejuvenation phase to celebrate reaching this phase and maintain his feeling of accomplishment. If he experiences temporary setbacks or feels a sense of being overwhelmed or disillusioned in the future, he will remember how it felt to be rejuvenated and understand how to get back to that point.

### Reflection

You could experience a reflection phase toward the end of the school year. In this phase, you may find yourself reflecting on the school year's positive and challenging aspects. You think about what went well and how you can duplicate those events, what didn't go so well and how you can make changes to avoid those problems, how you will start the next school year differently, and what you plan to do over the summer to get ahead.

The reflection phase is something those in other professions don't always get to enjoy. Because teachers get a chance to start over each school year, they have a built-in opportunity to think through their practice and make significant changes as needed.

Because of this unique opportunity to make significant changes, the reflection phase can be very beneficial. Following are some ideas and strategies to help you make the most of this phase.

▸ Anticipate that this phase will come at the end of the school year and give yourself time to engage in reflection.

▸ Talk with your mentor or coach about this phase. Ask him or her for ideas to help you reflect on your year and prepare for the upcoming school year.

▸ Consider asking your mentor to use formal questions to guide you in your reflections. Questions such as, "What do you think went well this year?" or "What do you want to change in your classroom for next year?" or "What do you want to make sure doesn't happen again next year?" help you to specifically focus your reflections on specifics that help a thriving new teacher clearly identify issues. General reflection questions may not provide this level of specificity.

▸ Develop preliminary plans to revise your teaching or specific classroom elements for the next school year. Even though most of the plan will be implemented over the summer, if you wait until then you may forget some of the improvements you are identifying through your reflections. Making some planning notes will help you as you work later to develop a more specific improvement plan.

▸ When reflecting, be sure to take a balanced approach by celebrating the good things you have accomplished as well as focusing on the things you want to change.

Let's see how our new teacher Antonio uses some of these strategies as he enters the reflection phase.

> *The school year is coming to a close for Antonio. He learned a lot during his first year, and he wants to make some changes for future school years. Antonio spends a couple of evenings writing some of his thoughts down in his journal. In his reflections, he is able to identify aspects that he wants to repeat during the next school year and some aspects he wants to improve. He is excited about the possibilities for the upcoming school year.*

> *He is so excited, in fact, that he asks his mentor, Hermine, to meet with him. During this meeting, he shares his reflections with her and asks for her thoughts on possible resources to help him. Hermine shares her perspective on Antonio's reflections and then identifies several resources he will find helpful as he works to make*

*changes for the upcoming school year. Antonio thanks Hermine for her ideas and support and tells her how helpful she has been as a mentor to him in his first year.*

In the example, we see how Antonio used the energy he gained in the reflection phase to help him plan for the future. Something else that is clear is the positive connection Antonio made with his mentor. Working with a mentor may sound like a common-sense strategy, but sometimes new teachers don't make full use of this resource. New teachers may try to keep others from knowing they are struggling. Thriving new teachers, however, work to develop and sustain good relationships with mentors and coaches in order to learn from them.

### Anticipation

Upon emerging from the reflection phase, you'll find you are feeling optimistic. You are probably feeling like you have conquered some of the challenges you faced during your first year as a new teacher and are now ready to move forward. As you think about moving forward, you may be experiencing some of the same feelings you had during the first anticipation phase. Even though you are in another anticipation phase, you may view it a little differently this time around. You now have a more realistic view of the challenges and opportunities in teaching. You may think about the students, parents, and families differently since you know many of them. With this more realistic view, some new teachers find that they approach issues with a little more caution than before. Be careful that this caution doesn't make you become too skeptical. Skepticism can lead to negative feelings that can impact your attitude and ultimately your professional experience. Be realistic but stay optimistic as you enter this new anticipation phase.

## Thoughts About the New Teacher Phases

The new teacher phases resemble a sequential cycle, though the phases may not always unfold in the same manner or on the same schedule for every new teacher. Keep the following in mind as you encounter the phases.

▸ You may not be alone in your thoughts and feelings. The new teacher phases are not just experienced by new teachers. Other more experienced teachers may experience these phases as well as they go through the school year.

▸ Some teachers may experience the various phases at different intensities than their colleagues.

▸ The amount of time teachers spend in the various phases may vary.

▶ Teachers may experience several different cycles of the phases during a school year. For example, a teacher may have multiple experiences moving between the survival and disillusionment phases before emerging to move into the reflection and anticipation phases. Going back and forth between several stages may be normal.

## Planning for the Phases

The planning template in figure 1.2 will assist you as you go through the various phases as a new teacher. It provides a visual method to keep track of your efforts and practices and helps you keep an objective, less emotional focus.

**Directions:** Use this template to help you plan to work through the various phases you may encounter as a new teacher.

| Phase | Feelings You're Experiencing in This Phase | Strategies to Help You During This Phase | Results of Your Strategies |
|---|---|---|---|
| Anticipation | | | |
| Survival | | | |
| Disillusionment | | | |
| Rejuvenation | | | |
| Reflection | | | |
| Anticipation | | | |

Write any final reflections you may have related to the phases and your first-year experiences with them.

Figure 1.2: New teacher phases planning and reflection template.

*Visit **go.solution-tree.com/instruction** to download a free reproducible version of this figure.*

## Mindset and Self-Perception

Your mindset and self-perception can make or break your first experience as a teacher. If you believe that you have the skills and ambition to do this job, you will be successful. If you let self-doubt and discouragement creep in, you may be programming yourself for failure. Reflect on the reasons you were hired: the strengths you possess, your experiences student teaching, your practicum experiences, and the other experiences—as a camp counselor, as a summer youth program leader, and so on—you have had that have prepared you to be a teacher. Many new teachers start out very confident but lose confidence over the course of the first year.

It's important to build your understanding of your strengths before you encounter these phases where confidence can diminish. One way that thriving new teachers build their confidence is by taking stock of their strengths and the areas with which they might struggle. Figure 1.3 provides a template for you to write your reflections before you begin the start of the school year. By using a form such as this as you are reflecting, you may become more aware of the strengths and interests that enabled you to go into teaching in the first place. By reflecting on your strengths in particular before the start of the school year, you can then revisit them later when you encounter challenges. Reflecting early helps to build a foundation so you feel grounded when you feel overwhelmed later.

| Directions: List your areas of strength and challenge and reflect. | | | |
|---|---|---|---|
| **Areas of Strength** | **Evidence of Strength** | **Areas of Challenge** | **Evidence of Challenge** |
| | | | |
| | | | |
| | | | |
| | | | |

After completing the template, take a few minutes to reflect on the following.

1. What trends or patterns did you notice as you reviewed your strengths? Which of these trends or patterns are the most important for your future success? How do you plan to access and enhance these areas of strength as you continue your teaching?

2. What trends or patterns did you notice as you reviewed your challenges? What areas of strength could you access to help overcome your challenges? What are your plans to address and overcome the challenging trends or patterns as you move forward?

3. When do you plan to revisit the strengths and challenges that you have identified in this exercise? How will you measure your growth as you make progress throughout your first school year?

Figure 1.3: Template for reflecting on strengths and challenges.

*Visit go.solution-tree.com/instruction to download a free reproducible version of this figure.*

## Sources of Information for Self-Reflection

Sometimes our thoughts and perceptions about our strengths and challenges are accurate; at other times, they are not. It can be helpful to check with others to see how they perceive you, your strengths, and your limitations. This information may be helpful as you identify your criteria for success. Some of these sources are discussed in the following section.

### Your Principal

It may seem intimidating to talk with your principal—especially since he or she will be evaluating your performance. You may want to schedule some time before the school year to talk about your strengths and challenges. Your principal may have gathered information about your strengths and limitations during the interview process that could be helpful for you to know. As your principal has come to know you better, he or she may have gained more insight about you that will be helpful to discuss as you approach the upcoming year. Your principal may also have information about your students that you may find helpful in your planning for the start of school. For example, during the selection process, he or she may have noticed how quickly you built relationships with students, how your skill set was a good match with your department or grade level, or how you demonstrated your knowledge of the instructional content. All of these strengths may be helpful in working with a particular group of students. Your principal can help you match these strengths and set goals for improvement.

Take notes as your principal shares his or her perceptions, and then when you are in a setting in which you can reflect, think about the evidence your principal used to come to these conclusions. Be sure to add this information to your reflection journal.

### Your Mentor or Instructional Coach

As mentioned previously, new teachers are often assigned mentors, coaches, and other peers who can help them make a successful transition into the classroom. If you have such a support person, he or she may have had an opportunity to meet with you or see you teach, or had conversations with your principal or the selection committee that was involved in your hiring. Mentors, instructional coaches, and other professional peers may have extensive knowledge of your areas of strength and some challenges you will face. Schedule a meeting with your peer support staff member and ask him or her to share some preliminary thoughts related to your successes and challenges. Keep notes during this conversation and transfer the information to your reflection journal or template.

### Your Job Description

You can gain valuable insight into your strengths and the challenges you face by reflecting on the job description for your position. Even if the job description is general, you will still find some details that can be helpful to you as you are taking stock of your strengths and challenges. For example, a job description that states that the teacher will gather and utilize assessment information to help students achieve success lets you know that this will be an important aspect of the job.

### Your District's or School's Teaching Performance Standards

In *Score to Soar: Moving Teachers From Evaluation to Professional Growth* (Eller & Eller, 2015), we discuss the importance of schools providing clarity in the standards they use to evaluate teacher performance. Clear performance standards enable teachers to have a good understanding of the criteria that will be used to evaluate their teaching performance. Carefully review the teaching performance standards for your district. As you review them, think about how your strengths fit into these standards and in which areas you may need to grow to meet expectations. For example, if one standard relates to effective classroom management and you think you are strong in developing good relationships with students, you would want to think about how you'll use this skill in helping you address this teaching standard. As you generate examples, add these to your journal or reflection template.

## Scope of Control

Remember that there are some issues that are within your scope of control and some that are not. You can control your attitude toward students, your lesson pacing, and your use of motivational techniques, for example. You can make changes within these areas to maximize your success.

On the other hand, there are aspects related to teaching that are outside of your scope of control. These could include, for example, student and parent attitudes, the experiences students have prior to coming to your classroom, and students' academic level. Since these are beyond your scope of control, it may be impossible or very difficult to change them.

Understanding what's within and outside your scope of control is very important to your emotional well-being and success as a teacher. In many cases, new teachers try to impact all aspects of their students' lives. They find themselves agonizing over things they can't control, and it's easy to feel sad and start to worry. This can lead to deeper sadness and even depression, which can negatively impact your mindset and your performance as a teacher.

In the book *The Seven Habits of Highly Effective People*, author Stephen R. Covey (1989) uses the terms *circle of concern* (the issues people are concerned about that may be outside of their scope of control) and *circle of influence* (the issues people may be concerned about that are inside of their scope of control). Covey's contention is that we need to spend time on those issues that are within our scope of control—in our circle of influence—and minimize the time we spend worrying about or trying to change the issues that are inside our circle of concern, which means outside of our scope of control.

Consider the following example.

> *Melanie, a middle school mathematics teacher, has been dealing with a particularly difficult situation in her classroom. Each afternoon, as the fourth-period students enter the classroom, there is chaos and disarray. Students are slow to take their seats, pushing, shoving, and bumping into each other. Melanie has to monitor students and remind them to come in and sit down. This becomes frustrating and wastes valuable time that she could be using in her teaching. Melanie becomes upset and feels negatively toward her students because they cannot enter her classroom in an organized manner.*

> *Melanie remembers reading about the concept of scope of control and decides to see if this concept might help her. She asks her mentor, Phillip, to meet with her to talk about analyzing the situation. Melanie shares her perceptions, and she and Phillip work on completing the template in figure 1.4 (page 24). Phillip then talks with Melanie about how she can focus on the aspects within her scope of control. Phillip shares some resources that Melanie can implement to begin to address the challenging situation.*

> *Melanie's mentor suggests that Melanie think about designing a better process for the students to enter her classroom, and then have an engaging activity ready for students when they enter. These strategies are within her scope of control. Melanie then examines the situation objectively and notices that several other things are getting in the way of students entering her classroom and getting right to work. First, she notices that some desks are partially blocking the door. This forces students to go around them, which impacts their ability to quickly get to their desks. Second, she notices that when the period starts, she is normally on the other side of the room dealing with attendance issues. The third thing she notices is that there are several students who are getting ready for class promptly, but they're waiting for Melanie to give them instructions on how to start. While they're waiting, they start to talk with other students and get off task.*

> *To improve the situation, Melanie moves the furniture blocking the classroom entrance. She also moves her computer closer to the classroom door so she can be near the entrance as she takes*

*attendance. Finally, Melanie posts an activity for the students to complete when they enter so they will be focused as she takes attendance, deals with students as they enter, and so on. After a couple of days of implementation, she begins to notice an improvement in how students enter her classroom and get right to work.*

---

**Directions:** Use this template as you examine issues in your classroom to determine what is within your scope of control.

1. List the issue or problem you are encountering.

   *The students are coming into the classroom in a disruptive manner.*

2. List any subissues related to the problem you are encountering.

   *Students are taking too long to enter. Students are pushing and shoving each other. Students who want to get to work are held up by the disruptive students. It's taking longer each day to start class. Since the class starts out chaotically, I'm noticing that it's easier for students to get off-task during the lessons.*

3. Using the following table, divide the subissues you listed into the categories of inside and outside of your scope of control.

| Issues Within Your Scope of Control | Issues Outside Your Scope of Control |
|---|---|
| • *Procedures for entering the classroom*<br>• *My reactions to the students when they don't enter properly*<br>• *The classroom furniture arrangement* | • *Student interest in sitting down and getting to work*<br>• *The past experiences students have in coming into classrooms*<br>• *Student reactions to my procedures while I am taking attendance* |

4. What are your plans to address the issue you identified in questions 1 and 2?

   *I need to change the procedures for starting class, such as providing an activity to engage students when they enter. I need to move furniture so there is a clear pathway to get in and out of the classroom. I need to state my directions positively rather than getting upset with the students.*

5. What did you learn from completing this exercise?

   *I learned that there are some simple things I can do to address the problem.*

---

Figure 1.4: Template for identifying aspects that are inside and outside of your scope of control.

*Visit **go.solution-tree.com/instruction** to download a free reproducible blank template of this figure.*

New teachers can apply the concept of scope of control to a variety of other situations beyond classroom management, such as:

▸ Student reactions to new processes

▸ Parent perceptions of your classroom, teaching, or handling of situations

‣ Student and parent reception of feedback

‣ Your peers' perceptions of how things are going in your classroom

‣ Your principal's reaction to an issue

‣ Other pertinent issues in teaching

When encountering challenges, be sure to reflect on your scope of control of the situation to help you make sense of the issue. Previously, we talked about the various phases you might encounter as a new teacher. While the strategy of identifying scope of control can be used in all of the phases, it may be particularly helpful in helping you move out of the survival and disillusionment phases. Consider using the concept of scope of control whenever you encounter issues that are difficult or provoke concern.

## Making a Good First Impression

Making a good first impression is something that is within your scope of control as a new teacher. When you are working to put together your classroom, make sure it reflects your professionalism as a teacher. For example, if your room is neat and clean, students will see that you care enough about them to make sure everything is in place to start the year. When you send messages to students and parents (either as hard copy or electronic), take a few minutes to review them to make sure the messages are clear, well written, and free of spelling and grammar errors, and accurately convey what it is you are trying to communicate. This extra attention to detail will help your students and their families form a good first impression of you.

In addition to making a good impression with your students and their families, you will also want to make a good impression with your principal and colleagues. After all, you'll be working with them extensively over the next school year (and hopefully beyond). If they have a positive impression of you, they will be more likely to be invested in your success as a teacher. If they find you aloof and abrasive, they will not be as committed to you. A new teacher's failure to get his or her contract renewed might have as much to do with personality and level of professionalism as with a lack of teaching skills.

## Understanding Your School, Community, and Students

Take some time as you prepare your classroom to learn about the community your school serves. Find out about the community background and priorities and its strengths and limitations. What are the community's sources of pride? What are its priorities? How does the community value education?

As you think about your students, try to determine what they will be like. Do they have common experiences? How have students performed academically? Do they have any special circumstances? Do they face any specific challenges or struggles? What can you expect from parental involvement? What is the diversity of the student population?

Many people who are drawn to education as a career are people who enjoyed school, admired their teachers, and probably had success as students. The students you serve, however, may not share the same experiences or attitudes in relation to school. Some of your students may have had negative school experiences or come from families where siblings or parents did not have good school experiences. They may not share your interest in the topic you teach. In fact, some may really dislike school or your content area.

This is important to keep in mind. Many new teachers are surprised by the attitudes and behaviors of some of their students. They can't understand why students don't like school or share their love for the content area. It is important that you consider what your students are like as learners and not only how you were as a learner. Your students may need to be motivated in different ways.

Step back and consider your content from your students' perspectives. This will help you design instruction that fits their needs. You might need to tap into your students' interest areas to get them motivated to learn your topic. You may want to consider using tools such as inventories, surveys, and so on to find out the interests of your students.

In addition to the students and community, you may also want to spend some time thinking about the school itself. Think about the school building, the reputation of the school, and other factors that will help you connect and become a part of the institution. For example, if the school has a poor reputation in the region, you may need to work harder to overcome that reputation and build confidence in your students and colleagues. If the building itself is old or outdated, you may need to think about how you'll organize your classroom activities based on these limitations. If the school has a rich reputation and history in the region, you may have to work harder to uphold that reputation. The time you spend thinking about the school will be beneficial as you connect with this school as a new teacher.

Use the template in figure 1.5 to help you as you begin to get to know more about your students and your community.

1. What is the school community like? What are the community demographics?

2. How does your community value education? How does it support education? What evidence do you have to back up your opinion?

3. Describe your students' backgrounds. How do they learn best? What kinds of activities seem to motivate them?

Figure 1.5: Questions for understanding your school, students, and community.

*Visit go.solution-tree.com/instruction to download a free reproducible version of this figure.*

## Peers and Colleagues

An important aspect of becoming a thriving new teacher is to connect with colleagues and build collaborative professional relationships. These kinds of professional collaborations will help you gain crucial knowledge and feedback about your work, plus allow you to share some ideas and strategies that may also help your peers. Many of your peers and colleagues have practical experiences working with your students and the other teachers in the school. You are going to find their experiences and information valuable.

In this section, we discuss forming relationships with mentors and coaches to develop yourself as a thriving new teacher. The following is a quick overview of each resource's role for a new teacher.

### Mentors

Mentors may be part of a process called *induction*—introducing new teachers to the processes, spaces, and culture of their new school. Mentors may focus on the technical aspects to help new teachers become familiar with things such as:

▶ School or district policies and procedures

▶ Supplies and materials

▶ Process for placing orders

▶ Process for entering grades

▶ Procedures for fire drills, disaster drills, lock down, and so on

▶ Attendance policies and daily management

▶ Instructions to operate the copy machine, building technology, and so on

▶ Building assessments, curriculum guides, and other district resources

### Coaches

The title *coach* can apply to a variety of people in supportive roles in a school. A coach is normally someone who is more focused on the teaching and learning process than the more technical aspects mentors support. Coaches are usually associated within a curriculum area. Coaches include:

▶ Mathematics coaches

▶ Reading coaches

▶ Instructional coaches

▶ Language arts coaches

Coaches are focused on issues related to curriculum, learning, teaching, and assessment. They will help you with the teaching part of your job.

Schools and districts may assign different tasks to mentors or coaches. They may also use different names or labels for colleagues designated to support new teachers.

### Making the Most of Your Interactions With Mentors and Coaches

Now that you know the differences between mentors and coaches, let's talk about how to maximize your relationships with them. If you are provided with one or both of these resources, you should think about how these people can support you. Consider using the templates in figures 1.6 and 1.7 to help organize your thoughts.

Also consider that some of the information you'll be told may not always fit you or your specific situation. The expression, "take it with a grain of salt" will help you maintain the proper level of skepticism to listen carefully but test any advice you receive against your own intuition and experiences.

## Ethics and Professionalism

The education profession is governed by a set of standards and ethics. Teachers are held to a high standard for their personal and professional behavior. States typically have a set of statutes that spell out these types of expectations. Also, educational institutions have developed ethical standards. Figure 1.8 (pages 30–31) shows an excerpt from the National Education Association (NEA; 2015) code of ethics.

| | **Directions:** Reflect on the following questions as you think about working with your mentor (or another supportive colleague). | |
| --- | --- | --- |

**Directions:** Reflect on the following questions as you think about working with your mentor (or another supportive colleague).

1. What aspects of building procedure do you know, and what aspects would you like to learn more about?

2. Which of the following areas do you understand how to do, and which things would you like assistance in learning more about?

| | **Know How to Do** | **Need Additional Information** |
| --- | --- | --- |
| • Operating the copy machine | ☐ | ☐ |
| • Obtaining necessary materials | ☐ | ☐ |
| • Operating building technology | ☐ | ☐ |
| • Understanding how to get a substitute teacher | ☐ | ☐ |
| • Completing required paperwork | ☐ | ☐ |
| • Getting to know other staff | ☐ | ☐ |
| • Other learning needs _____ | ☐ | ☐ |

3. What do you know in relation to school policies? What do you need to learn about the policies?

4. What else would you like to learn from your mentor?

Figure 1.6: Template for planning what you'd like to learn from your mentor.

*Visit **go.solution-tree.com/instruction** to download a free reproducible version of this figure.*

---

**Directions:** Reflect on the following questions as you think about working with your coach (or another supportive colleague).

1. What are the major learning outcomes within your curricular area?

2. What formative assessments are used to assess student progress in your curricular area?

3. Where are the curriculum pacing guides located?

4. What resources are available to support the curriculum?

5. What are the major teaching strategies associated with teaching the curriculum?

6. What other informational needs do you have in relation to the curriculum, your teaching, and so on?

Figure 1.7: Template for planning what you'd like to learn from your coach.

*Visit **go.solution-tree.com/instruction** to download a free reproducible version of this figure.*

**Principle I**

**Commitment to the Student**

The educator strives to help each student realize his or her potential as a worthy and effective member of society. The educator therefore works to stimulate the spirit of inquiry, the acquisition of knowledge and understanding, and the thoughtful formulation of worthy goals.

In fulfillment of the obligation to the student, the educator—

1. Shall not unreasonably restrain the student from independent action in the pursuit of learning.

2. Shall not unreasonably deny the student's access to varying points of view.

3. Shall not deliberately suppress or distort subject matter relevant to the student's progress.

4. Shall make reasonable effort to protect the student from conditions harmful to learning or to health and safety.

5. Shall not intentionally expose the student to embarrassment or disparagement.

6. Shall not on the basis of race, color, creed, sex, national origin, marital status, political or religious beliefs, family, social or cultural background, or sexual orientation, unfairly exclude any student from participation in any program, deny benefits to any student, or grant any advantage to any student.

7. Shall not use professional relationships with students for private advantage.

8. Shall not disclose information about students obtained in the course of professional service unless disclosure serves a compelling professional purpose or is required by law.

**Principle II**

**Commitment to the Profession**

The education profession is vested by the public with a trust and responsibility requiring the highest ideals of professional service.

In the belief that the quality of the services of the education profession directly influences the nation and its citizens, the educator shall exert every effort to raise professional standards, to promote a climate that encourages the exercise of professional judgment, to achieve conditions that attract persons worthy of the trust to careers in education, and to assist in preventing the practice of the profession by unqualified persons.

In fulfillment of the obligation to the profession, the educator—

1. Shall not in an application for a professional position deliberately make a false statement or fail to disclose a material fact related to competency and qualifications.

2. Shall not misrepresent his or her professional qualifications.

3. Shall not assist any entry into the profession of a person known to be unqualified in respect to character, education, or other relevant attribute.

4. Shall not knowingly make a false statement concerning the qualifications of a candidate for a professional position.

5. Shall not assist a noneducator in the unauthorized practice of teaching.

6. Shall not disclose information about colleagues obtained in the course of professional service unless disclosure serves a compelling professional purpose or is required by law.

7. Shall not knowingly make false or malicious statements about a colleague.

8. Shall not accept any gratuity, gift, or favor that might impair or appear to influence professional decisions or action.

*Source: Adapted from National Education Association, 2015, p. 435–436.*

Figure 1.8: Excerpt from the Code of Ethics of the National Education Association.

This code of ethics concentrates on two major themes: commitment to students and commitment to the profession. The first area deals with issues related to diversity, health and safety, student-teacher relationships, student learning, and so on. The second addresses ethical issues specific to the profession, including collegial confidentiality, accuracy in teaching experiences, personal benefits related to teaching, and others.

Once you have read the NEA's code of ethics, respond to the following questions.

1. What are some of the major points the NEA code of ethics outlines?

2. Which of these points were you aware of before you reviewed the list? Which of these points are new to you?

3. How do you plan to use the information you learned?

Standards of ethics such as the NEA's statement serve as a guide for educators. Take the time to learn these standards or the standards for your particular state. Taking the time to review and understand ethical standards could help you avoid a problem in the future.

## Summary and Reflection

In this chapter, we addressed some of the topics you'll need to consider as you start your work as a teacher. These foundational components of teaching will help you get a good start on your teaching career. They are also topics many people don't think about when they get started in teaching. As you review your learning from this chapter, reflect on the following questions.

▸ Why is it important to reflect on your strengths and limitations as a teacher? What are some sources of information you can use to help you as you examine these areas?

▸ How can the idea of scope of control help you as you approach your teaching?

▸ What are some of the main points of a set of professional ethics? Why are ethics important in our profession?

Now that you have some background information, it's time to think about how to get started. In chapter 2, we provide ideas and strategies to help you as you embark on the first year of your journey as a teacher—a rewarding and fulfilling career!

# Getting Off to a Great Start

*Jacob is getting ready for his first day teaching fifth grade. He has worked hard to get his classroom set up. As the students come in, Jacob is standing at the classroom door and greets each student personally, welcoming them to the classroom.*

*But Jacob feels like he already knows his students. This is not the first time they have met. During the summer, Jacob sent each student a letter introducing himself and asking if students and their parents (or other family members) would like to stop by the classroom to meet him. Most of the students took Jacob up on his offer. In addition, he learned detailed information about them from their parents and already knew some of their interests and areas of strength and weakness.*

*Jacob is expecting to have a great first day with his students because he has already spent time preparing and starting to build a rapport.*

Jacob's preparation went beyond just getting his classroom ready, reviewing the curriculum, and organizing his instruction. He also spent his time getting to know his students and their families. Getting off to a great start is crucial for your success as a new teacher. We've all heard the expression, "You don't get a second chance to make a first impression." This is very important in teaching.

All the ideas presented in this chapter will help you as you work to successfully launch your school year. They've been designed to help you establish a positive first impression with your students.

## Designing the Physical Space in Your Classroom

An important part of your success as a thriving new teacher is how you set up and organize your classroom space. Sometimes the classroom arrangement will depend on the physical size and layout of the space you have to work with and the desks or tables provided. In those cases, you'll be somewhat limited in how you can arrange your classroom. In other cases, you'll have the flexibility to set up the classroom in a manner that works best for you.

When designing your classroom, you want to examine and consider the following.

- Your preferred teaching style and methods
- The type of work or projects students will be completing in your classroom
- The amount of and type of movement that will be required within the classroom by yourself and your students
- How students can safely and efficiently enter and exit your classroom
- Student location in relation to supplies and materials (pencil sharpener, laptops or tablets, laboratory equipment, and so on)
- The location of power outlets for computers, projectors, and other electrical equipment
- The location of windows, heating and air-conditioning elements, and other features that may cause you or students to get extremely warm or cold
- Where you will work with students in small groups
- The location of any learning centers so traffic flow can be managed
- Where your desk will be located and the traffic flow in relation to your desk
- Where students can submit completed work and the traffic flow to and from this area
- The location of any fixed or attached furniture
- The location of a quiet study area where students can relax, read, or work in small groups
- The location of any emergency or alternative exits and the potential traffic flow out of the classroom in the event of an emergency

Following are some common classroom-design arrangements and some of the advantages and disadvantages of each (Eller, 2004).

## Traditional Classroom or Presenter Arrangement

This is a traditional arrangement for a classroom. The students are arranged into rows, and the teacher works from the front of the room where most instruction comes from. Figure 2.1 shows this arrangement.

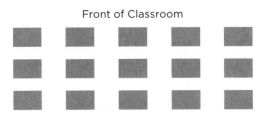

Figure 2.1: Traditional classroom arrangement.

This arrangement helps when most of the instruction comes from the front of the room. It promotes individualism and listening, and limits student interaction, which is helpful for classroom management. And there are travel lanes and paths to move around the classroom.

However, this classroom arrangement minimizes the opportunity for students to work together or in small groups. Students in the back of the room may lose focus or get off task. Students in the back may be far away from you and the board, and it may be hard for some students to see and hear.

This classroom accommodates teachers who prefer to present information, teach using a projector or SMART Board, or who want students to work individually.

## Half-Moon or Horseshoe Arrangement

In the half-moon or horseshoe arrangement, students sit around a center point. You may teach from the center or around the edges, but the attention is toward the middle of the room. Figure 2.2 shows this arrangement.

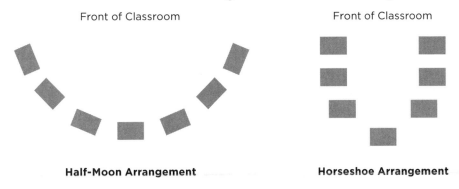

Figure 2.2: Half-moon and horseshoe arrangements.

With the half-moon or horseshoe arrangement, all students are close to the front (or center of the teaching). Most teachers do their teaching from the center of the horseshoe so they are relatively the same distance from all the students. Some teachers also walk around inside and outside of the horseshoe in order to keep in close proximity to their students. Since students are closer to one another, it's easier to hold group discussions, deliberations, debates, and so on. You can ask the students to talk to a partner without moving them. It's easier to use proximity control with the students because you are always within reach.

Unfortunately, in the half-moon or horseshoe arrangement, you are always visible to at least some of the students. This makes it harder to monitor students from the back of the room, which is possible with the traditional classroom or presenter arrangement. It's also easier for students to get off task and talk to their neighbors since they are so close together.

The half-moon or horseshoe arrangement works well if you like to present some information and then hold discussion with the large group. It can also accommodate you as you walk around the classroom during instruction.

### Circle or Oval Arrangement

In the circle or oval arrangement, all the students sit around a central focal point in a circle where the teaching takes place. Figure 2.3 shows this arrangement.

Figure 2.3: Circle or oval arrangement.

In the circle or oval arrangement, all students are close to the center of the teaching (if the teacher is in the center). This type of arrangement makes it easy to hold group discussions, deliberations, debates, and so on. It's also easy for the teacher to divide the students into two small groups to focus on sides of an issue or the pros and cons. Students can meet in partner groups easily, and the teacher can use proximity control to keep students on task.

However, the circle or oval arrangement makes it easy for the students to get off task and talk to others.

This type of arrangement works well if you don't depend on teaching from the front of the room. It can also be good if you share information using notebooks or tablets where students do not need to look to the front of the room. Teachers who present information and then hold discussion with the large group also find this arrangement helpful.

### Cluster Group Arrangement

In the cluster group arrangement (figure 2.4), students are divided into smaller groups.

Front of Classroom

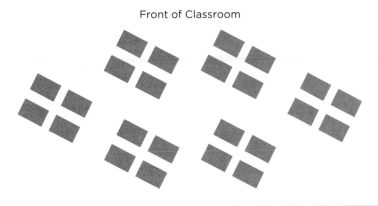

Figure 2.4: Cluster group arrangement.

In the cluster arrangement, it's very easy to conduct group work. Students can be divided into smaller groups and subdivided into even smaller units if needed. This arrangement also makes efficient use of classroom space since desks or work stations are connected. With the open spaces between the groups, a teacher can move easily around the classroom to manage student behavior plus monitor student progress in case extra help or reteaching is needed.

However, this arrangement has limitations. Since students are always sitting in groups, classroom management can become a challenge. Students can either talk to each other too much or troubles can arise if they do not like one another. You can mediate these challenges by putting careful thought into who is in each small group. Another limitation is that some students will always have their backs to you during instruction.

The cluster group arrangement fits well with teachers who like to present a small amount of information, then ask students to meet and talk about it. This arrangement also works well for cooperative learning, small-group work, and for other collaborative learning strategies. You can use this arrangement by coupling Smart Boards with tablets or notebooks (where students concentrate on their devices rather than having to look up front).

## Planning Your Classroom Arrangement

Use the template in figure 2.5 to help you as you plan for the classroom arrangement that makes the most sense for your teaching style and your students' needs.

---

**Directions:** Respond to the following questions to help you determine the optimal arrangement for your teaching style and your students' needs. Once you have reflected on the questions, draw a map of your classroom arrangement.

1. What kinds of instructional strategies do you plan to use in your classroom? Write the percentage you think you use each strategy during a typical week. Using the information from this exercise, select the classroom arrangement that will best accommodate the most common instructional strategies you use in your classroom.

   _____ Lecture, presentation

   _____ Small-group work, discussion, debates

   _____ Individual work and projects

   _____ Short presentations followed by note taking

   _____ Large-group presentation followed by work on a device (notebook or tablet, and so on)

   _____ Other

2. How well behaved are your students? What kinds of issues do you encounter with them during instruction and individual or group-work time? This aspect may be hard for you to determine definitively as a new teacher. You may get some ideas from your initial interactions with students before school starts or through conversations with your colleagues or mentor. If you have no idea what student behavior might be like, select classroom arrangements that will minimize interactions to start the year (for example, presenter).

3. Draw a map of your potential room arrangement.

4. Review your potential room arrangement. What issues might you encounter if you implement this arrangement? How could you prevent or overcome these issues to help make your arrangement a success?

---

Figure 2.5: Classroom arrangement planning template.

*Visit **go.solution-tree.com/instruction** to download a free reproducible version of this figure.*

Even though you have thought through many common issues related to classroom arrangement, take some time during the first few weeks of school to observe and evaluate how your arrangement is working. As you encounter unexpected issues, you may need to make some adjustments in your physical classroom plan. By making these adjustments, you will be maximizing the arrangement efficiency and the flow of students in, around, and out of your classroom. Many classroom-management issues have actually boiled down to problems with poor classroom arrangement. In some cases, moving furniture items increases the efficiency of traffic flow and can take care of a lot of problems that might be mistaken as behavior issues. Keep this in mind as you develop and refine your classroom arrangement.

## Introducing Yourself to Students and Their Families

To your students, you are a very significant person. You'll be spending quite a bit of time learning together. It's critical that you find ways to get to know them, their families, how they learn, what they are interested in, and other important information. The students you are working with may come from a variety of family structures. It's important to think about this as you work to build relationships. In this chapter, we may refer to those who are responsible for your students as parents, family members, or guardians. All of the strategies in this chapter can be successful with anyone who is the primary guardian of a student.

Thriving new teachers build relationships with their students and students' parents, guardians, and families. Before the start of the school year, consider writing a letter to students and parents introducing yourself and sharing some appropriate background information about yourself.

### Letter to Parents and Families

For elementary students, share with parents and families some information about yourself along with what the students will be learning and how you are very excited to be their child's teacher. Explain how parents can be a part of their child's education experience. One of the most important things elementary parents want to know is that their child will be safe and you have the student's best interest in mind—that you care about their child. Teachers should show that they have the "care factor"—a focus on the student more than the content. You should show that you have the students' best interest in mind and that you are student centered. The old expression, "People don't care how much you know until they find out how much you care" is applicable here. This is especially important for elementary age parents and should be reflected in your introduction letter.

For secondary students, share with parents some information about yourself, information about what students will be learning, your expectations, how you might be assessing their child, and how you will be supporting their children. Since parents want the best for their children, don't forget to mention that you are very excited to be their child's teacher. This is important because parents know that teachers who like what they do will likely have a good relationship with their students. They need to see from how you describe your interest in working with students that you have their child's best interest at heart.

It is also important to share your desire to have open communication between school and home in your first exchanges with parents. You might explain how parents can be a part of their child's education experience by working with him or her at home, keeping in touch with you, sharing information they think might be helpful to you, and asking you questions as the year progresses.

When asking parents to share information about their child with you, provide some prompts in your letter to guide parents, such as asking what their child's strengths and weaknesses are, how they think their child learns best, and what their child's special interests are. Your letter will be your first contact with parents, so make sure you include all the essential elements to give a great first impression. Figure 2.6 shows a sample letter to parents.

Dear Mr. and Mrs. Anderson,

Welcome to fifth grade! I am looking forward to getting to know you and your child and working together to help your child succeed. As parents and guardians, I understand that you are the most important teachers in your child's life. You and I both play a critical part in our partnership to support your child achieving the goals set forth in fifth grade. I have written an introduction letter to your child about myself, but I would like to take this opportunity to give you a brief overview about me, my background, and experiences as well.

I earned my bachelor of science in elementary education at Iowa State University and my master's in education at Arizona State University. I am a new teacher here at Kennedy Elementary School; however, I student taught in both second and fourth grades.

I will be teaching your child reading, writing, language, spelling, science, and social studies. As I stated in your child's letter, I love all of the subjects that I teach, but it is especially my passion to instill a lifelong love of reading and writing in all of my students. I have very high expectations of myself as a teacher as well as of my students. I have always found high expectations with support to be a formula for success! I want this to be an enjoyable year for all of my students but also a productive, challenging, and encouraging year.

In addition to providing you with some information about me as a teacher, I would like to get to know more about my students before the school year starts. I'm asking all my students' parents to write me a one-page letter about their child. In this letter, please address the following:

- Your child's interests
- Two to three strength areas for your child
- How you think your child best learns
- Anything else you think that would be helpful for me to know in working with your child this year

The letter can be handwritten or typed, whatever works best for you. I have included a self-addressed, stamped envelope for you to use in returning the letter to me. Please return the letter by August 27.

I will use the information you provide in the letter to get to know your child and plan our first few days together. I will not share the information you provide with any other teacher or your child (unless you want me to).

In addition to this letter, if you have any other concerns, please feel free to contact me. Communication is a huge part of your child's success. If you have any questions or concerns, would like to visit our classroom, schedule a conference, or volunteer to help out, you can contact me by phone at the school number listed on this letterhead, extension 32.

Once again, welcome to fifth grade! I know that together we can make this a wonderful school year.

Sincerely,

Mrs. Pedersen

Figure 2.6: Sample letter to parents and guardians.

In figure 2.6, the teacher kept the letter focused and concise but also conveyed a positive message. The teacher also provided specific information and rationale for the letter she is asking parents to write. Since the parents don't know the teacher yet, it's important that she lets them know who will see their letter and what she plans to use it for in her classroom.

Figure 2.7 shows another sample parent letter so you can see how a different teacher approached the task. This letter is more concise than the previous one.

Dear Parents,

I am writing to ask you to become a partner with me in your child's education. I will only have your child for a short time, so I want to make a contribution that will last a lifetime.

I know my teaching must begin with making students feel at home in the classroom and helping all students come together to form a learning community. This classroom community is made up of unique individuals, each with his or her own learning style, interests, history, hopes, and dreams.

Figure 2.7: Second sample letter to parents and guardians.  Continued ➦

Would you please help me by taking a moment to write about your child? What is your child like? What are his or her interests? What are his or her hobbies? What are things you know, as a parent, that would be important for me to know? I want to know how your child thinks and plays. How do you see your child as a learner and as a person? Please use the attached envelope and send in your response by Friday, August 30.

Thank you for your cooperation. I look forward to a wonderful partnership in your child's education.

Thank you!

Mr. Wilson

You might also want to include in your letter to parents your thoughts about a parent-teacher communication plan (as in figure 2.8). This plan should set clear, consistent, and high expectations for performance in class. This will put parents on your side and enable them to reinforce your expectations at home.

In my classroom, I plan to reach out and communicate with you:

- When we are starting a new unit of study
- At least twice each quarter with information related to your child's achievement
- When I notice a change in your child or his or her behavior
- When your child shares something that is troubling him or her
- When I feel that I should inform you about something or when we should work together to address an issue or situation

As a parent, I encourage you to contact me when:

- You have a question about something that happened in school
- Your child brings home a note or an assignment that needs clarification
- Your child shares something about my classroom or the school that is troubling
- You feel that you should inform me about something or when you think we should work together to address a situation or issue

Figure 2.8: Sample parent-teacher communication plan.

By having ongoing communication with parents, teachers learn more about student needs and students' home environment, which helps teachers have a clear understanding of their students. In addition, good communication helps to address issues before they get out of hand. When you reach out to parents you communicate to them that they are an important part of their child's education. All these outcomes result in you being able to do a better job and stay motivated.

## Letter to Students

We spent time discussing the importance of sending a letter to parents and families before the start of the school year. It is also important to connect with your new students. One way to do this is to send them a postcard or a letter introducing yourself and sharing with them how excited you are to have them in your classroom. Students love receiving mail—especially from their new teacher. Share information about yourself on an age-appropriate basis. All students will be interested in knowing details about you—where you are from, if you have any pets, if you are married and have any children, your favorite subjects and hobbies, and so on.

Another idea is to write a letter to students before the start of the school year telling them about you and then asking them to write you a letter back. Provide each student with a self-addressed, stamped envelope to send their letter. These letters will help you learn about your students, as well as about their writing ability. Once you receive the letters, begin to personalize your classroom around your students' interests, hobbies, books they like to read, and their families. Figures 2.9 and 2.10 (page 44) show samples of letters to students.

August 10

Dear Carlos,

Hi! My name is Ms. Carlson, and I will be your second-grade teacher this year at Wilson Elementary School. I am so excited that you will be in my class this year! I can't wait to meet you and start our year together. I know you are going to love second grade.

I live in the district with my husband, John, and we have four children, three boys and one girl. Their ages are fifteen, thirteen, ten, and eight years old. We also have a golden retriever named Monty. Our family loves to go camping, hiking, and swimming, and to play sports together. I personally love to read, write, and exercise every day.

I look forward to seeing you on the first day of school.

Sincerely,

Ms. Carlson

Figure 2.9: Sample letter to elementary students.

Dear Brianna,

Hello. My name is Mr. Lolatta. I will be your new sixth-grade teacher this year at Andersen Elementary. I'm really looking forward to meeting you and working with you.

Let me tell you a little about myself. I recently graduated from Cal State, Fullerton. I like to hike and camp. I have a black Labrador retriever named Rex who also likes to hike. We just finished a camping trip to the Grand Canyon. I'll fill you in on this trip and some of the funny things that happened when we meet in class.

I'm excited for the upcoming school year. I have a lot of interesting and fun units planned for you. I like to use activities that involve and engage you in the learning. I'm sure you'll enjoy them and find them helpful in your learning!

I'd like to get to know a little more about you before we start the school year. Please complete the questions at the bottom of this letter and send them back to me by August 20th. I'll use the information you send to plan our first week of learning together.

Thank you!

Mr. Lolatta

--------------------------------✂--------------------------------------------

Please write your name here: _____

What are your favorite subjects in school?

_____

_____

What types of books do you like to read?

_____

_____

What do you like to do when you have free time?

_____

_____

What questions do you have for me? What else would you like to know about me? (I'll answer some of these questions on the first day of school.)

_____

_____

Thank you for taking the time to write back to me. I'm looking forward to seeing you on the first day of school, August 27th.

Figure 2.10: Sample letter to students asking for a reply.

This sample letter is short but models how to reach out to students to help them feel more comfortable for the first day of school. Mr. Lolatta's questions are clear and focused, requiring short answers. To facilitate the students returning the letters, Mr. Lolatta includes a self-addressed, stamped envelope. After a reasonable amount of time, he contacts students who have not yet returned their responses. Some teachers offer incentives for returning the responses such as entry into a drawing on the first day of school.

Even though secondary (high school, middle school, and junior high) teachers work with many more students, it is still important for your students to get to know you. In addition to a letter to students, secondary teachers might include a more detailed website introduction students can access. An example of a completed postcard for secondary students is shown in figure 2.11.

---

Dear Ashley,

My name is Mr. Rodriguez, and I'm going to be your eighth-grade teacher this year. I'm excited to be able to teach you and for our year to get started.

We have lots of exciting things planned. I've set up a website so you can look at information about me and some of the interesting projects we are going to do this year. The address is www.mrrodriguezsclass.edu. Please take a look at it if you have time. Also, I'd like to get a chance to meet you and your parents before the start of the school year. On the website, I have set up a meeting schedule. Please set up a time to meet with me using this schedule.

I'm looking forward to meeting you!

Mr. Rodriguez

---

Figure 2.11: Sample postcard to secondary students.

## Teacher Website

Teachers can use their websites to introduce themselves and the course to students as well as to keep students and families updated about course- or grade-level content, homework, announcements, and so on. Websites should have the following elements.

▶ **Clarity:** The page should be neatly organized and readable, not crowded, and easy to navigate.

▶ **Essential information:** Posted information must be accurate and easy to find, and important for both students and parents.

▶ **Parent- and student-friendly resources:** These elements include resources like a calendar, a language translator, and links for additional information.

▶ **Appealing and professional design:** Teacher websites should be colorful and attractive, and they should always be professional.

These are only a few of the elements to consider when developing a website. Talk with your principal, technology support staff, mentor, and colleagues to find ideas you like when developing your classroom website.

# Making the Most of Events at the Start of the School Year

In this section, we present several examples of events schools may offer for families at the start of a school year. These family events provide you with an opportunity to make a great first impression with the families or parents of your students. Keep in mind that your particular school will not offer every type of event or refer to them using the same names we have used in this chapter. We describe a variety of events to help you prepare for the one or two that your school might offer.

## Open House

A very traditional family event scheduled by many schools is an open house. Some schools schedule open houses before the first day of classes, while others schedule their open houses during the first few weeks of school. Some open houses are designed for parents, family members, and students to attend, while others are only for adults. Regardless of who attends and when an open house occurs, you will have the opportunity to meet parents and families and for them to get to know you. An open house also provides parents and families with the opportunity to learn about what will be happening in your classroom during the school year. To have a successful open house, it is important to invest time in planning for the event.

### Welcome Materials

At the open house, you want parents and families to feel welcomed and involved. One strategy that teachers have used to help parents feel connected is to have a welcome letter on each student's desk or table. In this letter, include everything you want parents to see and experience during the open house event. Sometimes, these letters are written by the teacher to the parents. In a teacher-authored letter, include a short welcome message, an overview of the upcoming school year, and other classroom information and details. Provide parents with a folder containing the various forms that they need to complete and return to the office, such as contact information, emergency forms, volunteer forms for field trips, and any other form you or the school thinks would be helpful in gathering parent and family information. Provide trays or baskets for parents and families to turn in the forms upon completion. Provide another folder of information that parents can keep, such as a copy of your schedule, a business card with your contact information (or a school information refrigerator magnet), a list of books at their child's grade level to read with their child (primarily for elementary students), and any other information you think would be helpful to them.

This idea of providing folders might be better for elementary classrooms where one teacher is primarily responsible for a group of students. In a secondary school setting, the forms might be collected by a homeroom teacher or by the school office staff at a separate work station provided at the open house.

### Parent and Family Activities

Include activities during the open house that engage families while helping them to connect with their students or learn about the school. One activity is to provide parents and family members with a form on which to write a letter to their child (used primarily if the open house is only for parents). Parents leave the letter in their child's desk for the student to find the next morning. Students love to find these letters and read what their parents think about them, their classroom, and the upcoming school year. While this may seem like a strategy that may be only used for elementary students, even middle school or junior high students enjoy getting a letter from their parent. At the middle school or junior high level, parents can put the letter or note in their child's locker.

If parents and students attend the open house together, you can also hold a scavenger hunt to help orient them to your classroom and school. Figure 2.12 (page 48) is a sample form for a scavenger hunt that features a variety of fun activities to help families get to know more about your classroom or school.

One activity described in the form in figure 2.12 is taking a picture of the student and his or her parents or family members (taken by a school volunteer on the night of the open house). You can use this picture later on a bulletin board featuring information about each student. Other scavenger hunt items that parents and students can seek out together include different stations in your classroom, such as the reading center, the mathematics center, and the classroom library. They can also tour the school to locate the restrooms, office, library, gym, cafeteria, music room, art room, and the classrooms of other teachers they may have during the school year. This scavenger hunt will help your students become more comfortable finding their way around the school and provide a way for parents to see the entire school.

**Directions:** Welcome! I have designed this scavenger hunt to help you get to know our classroom and school and some of the procedures and processes your child will be using this year. Please take a few minutes to complete as many of the activities listed on the form and visit as many places as you can.

| Have your picture taken with your family. | Visit the reading center. | Visit the mathematics center. | Find the supplies: stapler, tape, and pencil sharpener. | Find the location where students turn in homework. |
| --- | --- | --- | --- | --- |
| Visit the restrooms. | Visit the library. | Visit the cafeteria. | Visit the gymnasium or PE area. | Visit the art room. |
| Visit the computer lab. | Visit the music room. | Visit the office. | Visit the principal. | Visit the school secretary. |
| Visit the science room. | Visit the band room. | Visit the orchestra room. | Visit the nurse's office. | Visit the playground or recess area. |

Figure 2.12: Sample scavenger hunt form.

*Visit **go.solution-tree.com/instruction** to download a free reproducible blank template of this figure.*

As you develop the scavenger hunt, be sure to keep in mind that you want parents to actively engage in activities that will help them get to know you and the processes that you use in your classroom.

## Parent Information Night

Some schools offer a slight variation to the open house. This is typically called a parent information night. A parent information night is generally a little more formal and includes more specific classroom procedures and curriculum information than an open house. Some parent nights allow parents and family members to follow the daily schedule of their student. In this section, we describe information related to this more focused type of information night where teachers present information to a group of parents for about an hour. If you are participating in a more formal parent information night, consider including the following in your presentation:

▸ A welcome message and a self-introduction that includes information about your background, interests, and so on

▸ Your webpage and how to access the information on it

▸ An overview of the essential classroom procedures

▸ The daily schedule

▸ A list of the necessary school supplies for students

▸ Your classroom goals and expectations for students

- Examples of typical homework assignments and homework policies
- An overview of your grading policies and procedures
- Your discipline expectations and policies
- How parents can access students' grades
- How parents can volunteer in the classroom
- How parents can contact you
- How parents can get messages to their child during the school day
- Your cell phone use policies
- Examples of ways students can become involved in school (clubs, sports, co-curricular activities, and so on)
- Resources that are available for students to get help with their work
- Information about field trips, including transportation (buses), the lunch options and procedures, and other important information
- Other important aspects of your classroom (including your teaching methods, methods of assessment, safety drills, electronic devices used in the classroom, and so on)

At the end of the parent information night, be sure to provide time for parents to ask questions and mingle.

As with the open house strategy, it's a good idea to have a plan in place for parent or family information nights. See how a thriving new teacher, Jun, applies this idea for her parent information night:

> Jun, a new high school science teacher, is getting ready for her first parent information night. She wants to provide parents with pertinent information about her policies and procedures to make sure they understand her classroom expectations, how she will conduct her classes, how to use her classroom website, how parents can contact her, and other essential information parents may need for the upcoming year. She also wants to use this opportunity to build her credibility with parents. She develops an agenda for this parent information night (see figure 2.13, page 50).

**Objectives for the parent information night:** Parents will understand the major processes and procedures I use in my classroom. Parents will learn how I plan to organize the content and communicate with them about their children. I will establish credibility as a teacher with parents.

| Agenda Item | Time line | Method |
|---|---|---|
| 1. Introduce myself and share background. | 5 minutes | Presentation |
| 2. Share the classroom procedures and processes. | 5 minutes | Handout and presentation |
| 3. Show parents how to access grades online. | 5 minutes | Smart Board |
| 4. Show parents the school and the classroom webpages. Show them how to access information on each. | 5 minutes | Smart Board or projector |
| 5. Outline typical unit processes. | 5 minutes | Unit one syllabus |
| 6. Discuss parent-information processes (ways parents will receive information). | 5 minutes | Handout |
| 7. Share methods parents can use to contact me. | 5 minutes | Handout |
| 8. Respond to parent questions. | 5 minutes | Open discussion |
| 9. Talk informally with parents. | 10 minutes | Informal mingling, parents looking at classroom displays, and question cards |

**Materials and equipment needed:** Handouts of the unit one syllabus, handouts of the classroom procedures and classroom discipline expectations, handouts showing screenshots of accessing the grading program, Smart Board or computer, and question cards

Figure 2.13: Sample agenda for parent information night.

*Visit **go.solution-tree.com/instruction** to download a free reproducible blank template of this figure.*

*Jun's parent information night lasts about fifty minutes. This allows her about ten extra minutes at the end of the session to talk personally with several parents who stay later to share information about their children or to ask more in-depth questions. As a part of the materials she provides to parents and family members, she includes question cards. These question cards give parents an opportunity to write any questions they may have that they were not able to ask during the information night so Jun can review them and get back to parents later. She plans to respond to most of the questions by email or phone. Responding to these questions will enable Jun to start to build a relationship with parents.*

## Intake Conferences

Another parent and family information or communication strategy that some schools elect to use is an intake conference. This is different than the open house and family information night because an intake conference is normally designed as an opportunity for a teacher to listen while the parents or family member provide information about their child. Intake conferences usually occur before the start of the school year or within the first month of school.

An intake conference is an opportunity for you to get to know a student and his or her family. In order to make the most of the opportunity, it's a good idea to think about the kinds of information you want to gain from an intake conference. Let's see how one thriving new teacher approaches the opportunity.

> Justin, a new second-grade teacher, is getting ready for the start of his first year of teaching. As he prepares for the start of the school year, he asks himself questions such as:
>
> - What information do I need to know in order to do a good job with my students this school year?
>
> - What are the ways that my students learn best?
>
> - What things may have happened to my students over the summer that might impact their learning?
>
> - What have the parents learned in raising their children that might be helpful to me as their teacher?
>
> Luckily, Justin works in a school that uses an intake-conference process called early bird conferencing. In this process, the teachers hold a conference with the parents before the start of the school year to obtain information about their students, rather than just telling the parents about their students (as we do in typical parent-teacher conferences).
>
> Since the focus of the early bird conferences is to help Justin learn more about the students he will teach, he uses the questions he asked himself about his students to generate a series of questions he can ask parents and family members. He decides to provide a handout so parents and family members can respond to his questions before the meeting.
>
> By sending questions to the parents in advance, Justin finds that they are able to provide a lot of important information about their children. Because of what he learns, he better understands his students and has better insight into their learning needs and behaviors.

An example of the questions Justin used with parents and family members during the early bird conferences is included in figure 2.14.

The questions that Justin asks during his intake conferences are only a few of the many options a teacher could ask. The following is a list of questions you may consider asking parents.

▶ What are some of your child's favorite things to do when he or she has free time?

▶ What is your child's favorite subject in school?

▶ Who are some of your child's closest friends at school?

▶ What kinds of tasks do you feel your child does best?

▶ Does your child like to work in groups or by him- or herself?

▶ What are some of your child's favorite books?

▶ What are some of your child's hobbies?

▶ What is your child's favorite game?

▶ What are your goals for your child for the upcoming year?

▶ What are your specific goals for your child in mathematics and reading for the upcoming school year?

▶ What kinds of strategies did past teachers use with your child that were successful?

▶ How does your child manage projects and tasks?

---

**Directions:** Please take a few minutes to share your thoughts about the following during your intake conference with me. Your responses will be used to help me do a better job in working with your child this year. Your responses will be confidential and only used for my work with your child during the upcoming school year.

1. What are some things your child likes to do when he or she has free time?

2. What kinds of literature does your child read? What are his or her favorite books?

3. How does your child learn best? What ideas or strategies have worked for teachers who have been successful with your child in the past?

4. What are tasks that your child doesn't like to do? What has been successful in helping your child complete these tasks?

5. What do you think would be helpful for me to know in order to help your child have a successful year?

Thank you for taking the time to help me learn more about your child. We will have a successful year together!

---

Figure 2.14: Sample intake-conference questions.

*Visit **go.solution-tree.com/instruction** to download a free reproducible version of this figure.*

Intake conferences can be beneficial to you as a thriving new teacher. If your district does not implement intake conferences, you can conduct them on your own by doing the following.

▸ Discuss the idea with your principal. Get his or her perspective and feedback.

▸ Talk with your coach or mentor. Get his or her feedback and perspective.

▸ Set aside time before the start of the school year to meet with parents and family members. Consider offering options at a variety of times (morning, afternoon, and evening) to accommodate working family members. Be sure to also plan for your own safety and security when meeting with family members. For example, make sure other staff members are nearby if you are meeting with parents and family members outside normal school hours. Allow about thirty minutes for each meeting.

▸ Develop a letter describing the intake-conference process, questions for parents to complete, and ask parents to contact you and set a time to meet.

Figure 2.15 is a sample letter for parents to inform them of the intake-conferencing process.

---

Dear Parents,

I am interested in your child having his or her best experience this school year in my classroom. In order for this to happen, I need your help to share important information about your child.

During the week of September 15, I will be talking with every parent or guardian to gain your insight about your child. I'm calling these meetings intake conferences. During these intake conferences, I plan to listen to you to find out how your son or daughter best learns, what motivates him or her, what kinds of things he or she likes to do, how he or she has been successful with teachers in the past, and any other information you have gained over the years as his or her parent that you feel would be helpful.

Please complete the attached question sheet, and then contact me to set up a time for us to meet. You can contact me at my email address or by phone (both listed below my signature).

I'm looking forward to hearing your experiences and ideas when we meet in our intake conference.

Sincerely,

Mr. Sanchez

---

Figure 2.15: Sample letter introducing parents to the intake conference process.

Keep in mind that in an intake conference, you should focus on listening to what the parent has to say in relation to his or her child. Resist the impulse to share a progress report or add your own interpretation of the student. You'll want to make sure that you gather as much information from parents as possible during this intake conference.

### Parent-Teacher Conferences

An event that can cause anxiety and worry in new teachers is the parent-teacher conference. There are many ways to conduct parent-teacher conferences. Some schools have times scheduled for each parent, while others have a drop-in event. Your specific parent-teacher conference plan will depend on the type of conferencing your school uses, parent expectations, how conferences have traditionally been conducted, and many other factors. Before you prepare to plan for your first set of parent-teacher conferences, it is a good idea to get assistance from your principal, mentor, peer coach, or other colleague to assist you.

There are some considerations to keep in mind in relation to parent-teacher conferences. The following list outlines some of these items.

- Parents want to know that you understand their child and have the child's best interest at heart.

- Parents want clear and easy-to-understand information about how their child is doing, his or her strengths and challenges, and how the child can be successful in your classroom or content area.

- Parents want to know that things are fair in your classroom and that everyone can achieve success.

- Parents want honest information about their child presented in a tactful manner. Be honest, but don't be unnecessarily harsh in your assessment.

- Focus on their child. Don't talk about other children, how others are doing, or anything else that could be construed as gossip. At times, parents may try to get you to talk about other children. Stay professional and focused on their child.

- Be reasonable. Don't over or under promise. Share only what you think is reasonable and attainable. This will help you ensure that you are able to deliver on your promises.

- Be careful about negative comments from parents. Some parents may say negative things about their child, other children, or past teachers. If these kinds of comments come up, try to change the topic or bring up something positive. Don't engage in or give credence to these types of comments.

▸ Work to develop a partnership. Some parents seek a collaborative relationship with you to help their children be successful. Don't expect them to fix everything at home and don't take on issues that are out of your control. Developing a collaborative relationship will help you as you work with their child.

▸ Build on the positive. Every child has good things about him or her. Make sure that you spend time talking about the good in the child even if you have to also address difficult issues. Sometimes, starting off with good comments helps to set a positive tone that lasts through the conference. Ending on the positive also helps parents remember you as a positive person who is interested in the best for their child.

The parent-teacher conference is a prime opportunity for you to set up a collaborative relationship with your students' parents to maximize student success.

## Creating Your Schedule for the First Day of Class

Many teachers have a reoccurring dream where they are trying to teach but nobody is listening. In this dream, the students are out of control and no matter what the teacher does or says, the students are doing what they want. When the teacher wakes up, he can't believe it's a dream, and he hopes this scenario never becomes reality!

Your first day with students is an opportunity you will get only once. The tone you set on the first day in your class or classes is something that will stay with you during the entire school year. You'll want to use this day to set the tone, establish yourself as the teacher, get to know your students, set your expectations, and address other important aspects related to your teaching.

All teachers plan for their first day with their students based on their own personalities, their content areas, and the way they organize their classrooms. Even though there are differences in how each teacher plans, there are some common items to consider in preparing for that first day with your students.

▸ A "get to know each other" activity or team-building activities with the class

▸ General information about your background and experiences

▸ Your expectations for your students' behavior

▸ An overview of the topics and units the students will be studying

▸ The major learning processes or teaching methods you plan to use in the classroom

▸ Projects that the students might complete

▸ The schedule for the first week

▸ Major classroom procedures (getting materials and supplies, using the restroom, where to turn in homework, and so on)

▸ Information about the classroom webpage

▸ How you plan to help students learn and grow

The exact schedule you develop will depend on whether you will be teaching the students the entire day or whether you will be working with them for only a period. If you have your students for a whole day, you may be able to cover these items in one day. If you are only teaching the students for a period, it may take several days to relay all the information.

The following are some specific ideas by school level that you may want to include in your first day with students.

## Elementary

▸ Consider having the students help set up their learning environment. This creates ownership of the classroom and the learning environment.

▸ Plan a get-to-know-you activity.

▸ Do team-building activities with students.

▸ Have a morning meeting to get to know students and allow them to share what they did over the summer.

▸ Share the schedule for the day or week.

▸ Discuss processes and classroom procedures, such as checking out books from the classroom library, sharpening pencils, using the restroom, and where to turn in homework.

▸ Share the classroom webpage and how to locate it and navigate it.

▸ Share the seating chart.

▸ Share the process for taking attendance.

▸ Share your expectations for the organization of the student's desk and folders or notebooks.

▸ Assign textbooks to students.

▸ Share the expectations for movement in the classroom.

- Review information related to safety drills (fire, tornado, and lock-downs).
- Share your student expectations and rewards system.
- Discuss essential school supplies needed.
- Discuss the technology policy (computers and notebooks, cell phones, and so on).
- Explain the routines of the day.
- Share the designated area where you post daily or weekly assignments and the learning targets for each lesson.

## Secondary

- Consider having the students help set up their learning environment. This creates ownership of the classroom and the learning environment.
- Share the seating chart for students.
- Share the process for taking attendance.
- Conduct a get-to-know-you activity.
- Share the process for using a student planner.
- Share the process and procedure for school lockers.
- Share the process for hallway and restroom passes.
- Share how students can access their grades.
- Share any grading practices and policies.
- Share the best ways for students to communicate outside of class with you.
- Show the information that can be found on the school's webpage, how to locate the webpage, and other helpful webpage information.
- Review the course syllabus.
- Assign textbooks to students.
- Discuss the clear expectations for movement in the classroom.
- Review safety drills, such as fire, tornado, and lockdowns.
- Discuss the classroom expectations, the students' expectations of the class, and any rewards system.
- Share the cell phone and technology use policy.
- Share schoolwide expectations and procedures.
- Share the process for using lab stations.

You will find it helpful to actually develop a script to guide your discussion on the first day.

## Summary and Reflection

In this chapter, we have described some of the common elements of designing your classroom for success and getting to know your students and their parents. The strategies we have outlined in this chapter will help you set a positive tone and establish a good first impression with your students and their parents.

As you reflect on what you learned in this chapter, consider the following questions.

▸ How does your classroom set-up contribute to positive classroom management? What are some factors to think about as you design your classroom layout?

▸ What is the importance of reaching out to students and parents before the start of the school year? What are some aspects you need to remember in designing these early communications?

▸ What are some factors that are important to include in a parent open house? How do they contribute to a positive experience?

▸ Does your school conduct intake conferences? If it does not, is this something you plan on starting with your students? How is this approach helpful?

Once you have launched the school year and it's off to a great start, you'll want to continue your success. In chapter 3, you'll learn strategies to continue your success in the first weeks of school by building relationships with your students and their parents through solid communication strategies and goal setting.

# Building Relationships With Students

*LaShawn, a new elementary teacher, is conducting a morning meeting with her students. As each student shares what he or she did over the weekend, LaShawn listens carefully. She repeats a short summary of each student's contribution before asking the next student to share. As she repeats what the students told her, all of their eyes are focused intently on her. It is evident that the students know that LaShawn values what they have to say and has built a positive relationship with them.*

In this brief example, we see how the teacher used her listening skills to make sure she heard each student's contribution. When she summarized and repeated their comments, she was letting them know that she heard what they had to share. These are two important skills that teachers use to build positive relationships with their students.

There are many ways for new teachers to build emotional connections with their students. In this chapter, we focus on strategies for communication and goal setting and monitoring.

## Listen First, Tell Later

A skill crucial to building relationships with students is to listen first and tell later. When you wait to hear what students have to say before sharing your own opinion, you let them know that they are important and you are interested in understanding them and their thoughts. It's a common complaint of students that adults don't understand them and just want to tell them what to do. By putting your own opinion on hold and truly listening, you send an important message to your students: you signal to them that you are interested in what they think. Edgar Schein (1993) writes that to suspend means to set aside our perceptions, our feelings, our judgments and our impulses for a time and listen to and monitor our own internal experience and what comes up from within the group. Temporary suspension of opinion is an internal skill that allows the receiver of communication to withhold sharing an opinion about the message that was heard. Suspension is used to increase the opportunity of increased thinking and problem solving on the part of the sender. Presently, suspension is not used with much frequency in our society. We normally experience the opposite of suspension, cases where people are impatient with our thought process and who move in to give advice too quickly. This results in others finishing our sentences, prematurely giving their opinions and others not listening to our thoughts because they are busy formulating their own responses. When people use suspension, they are using it on a conscious basis for a selected period of time for the purposes of truly listening, understanding another perspective or to increase the problem solving capacities of the sender.

Temporary suspension of opinion is a strategic skill that requires much concentration on the part of the listener. It requires that the listener is really interested in listening to the sender of the message and understanding the sender's perspective (Eller & Eller, 2006).

Let's see how LaShawn uses the concept of suspension of opinion as she continues to work with her students.

> In her classroom, LaShawn talks with two students who are working together at an instructional center. The students seem somewhat confused with what they are supposed to do at the center. Even though LaShawn could just tell them the correct answer, she listens carefully and lets the students work through a solution to their question. Once they share their solution, LaShawn confirms their ideas and encourages them to move forward in relation to their work. The students seem to be motivated by the way LaShawn let them solve the problem, and they work hard the remainder of the time they are at the center together.

In this example, we can see how easy it would have been for LaShawn to just tell the students the answer to the issue they faced. Instead, she used suspension of opinion to keep from solving the issue and let them come up with their own ideas. Her patience and guidance showed them that she was confident in their abilities to solve issues. This helped her further develop her positive relationship with the students.

## Reflect on and Paraphrase What the Student Has Told You

When students tell you something, it is a good idea to acknowledge what they have said using reflecting or paraphrasing. Even though these strategies are similar, they do have some differences.

In paraphrasing, a teacher repeats back the student's general message as he or she perceives it. This perspective is confirmed with statements such as, "So what I hear you saying is . . ." or "If I understand you correctly, you are saying . . ." The *I* part of the message reinforces the teacher's perception. Some teachers find that using an I message helps them communicate their understanding in an indirect manner.

Some examples of paraphrasing statements include:

▸ "So if I heard you correctly, you were saying that you had difficulty completing the assignment."

▸ "From my perspective, you are telling me that you need more time to complete the task."

▸ "I heard you say that you worked hard and did a good job with the task."

▸ "It's my perception that you had a conflict with Jonah while you were on the playground."

Reflecting is similar to paraphrasing because the teacher repeats back what the student has told them; however, the language the teacher uses is more direct. A reflecting statement might sound like this: "You are saying that you are working hard on the project" or "Your main point is that you are distracted by the small group working near you." In both of these examples, the statement is direct and does not mention the teacher's perspective. Some teachers find they are more comfortable with the directness of reflecting.

Following are some examples of reflecting statements using the same content as the earlier examples to show the subtle language differences between paraphrasing and reflecting.

▸ "You had difficulty completing the assignment."

▸ "You're telling me that you need more time to complete the task."

▸ "You worked hard and did a good job with the task."

▸ "You had a conflict with Jonah while you were on the playground."

Whether you choose to paraphrase or reflect what students say to you, you'll find that the use of these skills will help you build positive relationships with your students.

## Avoid Autobiographical Communication

This skill is related to the earlier concept of listening. *Autobiographical communication* is communication in which the speaker is focusing on him- or herself and what he or she might do in a situation. For example, a teacher saying things like, "If it were me . . ." or "If I were you . . ." or "I hear what you are saying, now let me tell you about my situation . . ." takes the focus off the student and places it on him- or herself. When communicating with students, be sure to keep the focus on them and their situation. Nobody likes to be lectured to—particularly students. If you focus on them and their situations, you'll build rapport with them as well as show your desire to support them.

Keep in mind that while, in general, students may not like being told what to do, there are times when they may value you sharing your perspective related to situations and issues they are facing. If sharing your opinion will help a student who is encountering a difficult situation or in danger, you should intervene. If a student asks you for your opinion, it is also a good time to share. Using the skill of temporary suspension of opinion introduced previously may help you diagnose the situation and move forward based on the needs of each student.

## Establish and Maintain Appropriate Eye Contact

This strategy may sound like common sense, but we find that some new teachers can be so preoccupied by other things that they forget this fundamental aspect of relationship building. Also, in today's fast-paced world, many students regularly have conversations with adults in which the adults are constantly multitasking and are just too busy to stop what they are doing and really focus on what the student is saying. No matter how busy you are, be sure to stop and make and maintain eye contact when talking with students.

We specify that the eye contact be appropriate. This means that you should keep eye contact comfortable for the student. Be sure to take clues from your students when making eye contact. If they occasionally break eye contact to think or when formulating a response to you, follow their lead. If they are uncomfortable maintaining constant eye contact, possibly because of the norms of their culture or if they have confidence or self-esteem issues, model your eye contact after theirs to make them feel comfortable, inserting breaks in your eye contact as you talk with them.

Maintaining eye contact is something you can do as a teacher without insisting that a student maintain eye contact with you in a conversation. A student's break in eye contact could be for cultural reasons, or it could be the way the student handles emotional situations. For example, if a student seems to feel intimidated or embarrassed by a behavior or situation and looks away from you, continue to look at the student. You'll still communicate your interest in connecting, even if the student does not want to. The student may feel comfortable re-establishing eye contact after the emotional part of the conversation passes. Insisting on student eye contact when a student is uncomfortable may actually drive the student deeper into the negative emotional situation. Respect his or her reluctance, and you may find that the student will start to maintain eye contact as he or she builds rapport with you.

## Talk to Students About Topics of Interest to Them

A great way to build a relationship with your students is to talk about things that are of interest to them. If one of your students is in the school play, for example, you might ask about how the practices are going, what the student is learning by being in the play, or if she or he is successfully learning all the lines. If you have a student athlete, ask about the outcome of the last game, how the team performed, and the upcoming schedule. By talking about topics that interest your students, you show them that you are fascinated by them as people and want to build a more emotional connection and sound relationship.

## Keep Up With Current Trends

Whatever grade level you teach, recognize that you will need to become knowledgeable about current trends and topics of interest popular with your students. If you can show that you have some knowledge related to current trends, you are showing students that you are interested in them. You can gain this knowledge by listening to their informal conversations, asking friends' and relatives' children who are in the same age group as your students about topics of interest, watching popular television shows, and searching the Internet. When a topic comes up in your class that you are unsure of, listen carefully, and the students' conversation may give you some important clues. If you listen or even ask questions to help you increase your understanding of current trends, students will appreciate that you are taking an interest in their world.

## Welcome Students to Your Classroom

Welcome students to your classroom. This suggestion may seem like it should be common knowledge and everyone is already doing it. In our experience, we find that many teachers (especially new teachers) think they are too busy getting ready for the next class, managing attendance information, and talking to specific students to greet all students at the door as they come in the room.

By standing at the door and greeting your students at the beginning of a class or at the start of the day, you accomplish several things. First, you send a hospitable message. You are telling students that you are happy they are coming into your class and that you welcome them in. Second, you get to assess students' moods by watching how they respond. You can use this informal assessment to keep an eye on those students who seem to be upset, angry, worried, and so on. Third, you provide supervision of the hallways to ensure students are passing in an orderly fashion from class to class, using their lockers appropriately, and so on. Finally, you get to set the tone for the beginning of your class, which can help lead into a more smooth and focused time together.

## Know Students' Names and Use Them in a Positive Manner

In the beginning of the year, focus on quickly getting to know your students' names and then use them often in positive communication. If you are a new elementary teacher, this task might not seem too difficult, but if you teach secondary students, you may have 120–150 names to learn. It is important for you to find some way of getting to know your students' names. Some strategies include using assigned seating and keeping a seating chart for reference, using name tags or nameplates on students' desks or tables, and developing associations that help you remember students' names.

Let's see how Hernando, a new high school teacher, uses the idea of name plates to get to know his students.

> Hernando, a new social studies teacher, teaches six sections of history each day. Since he has so many students, he knows he will have trouble getting to know all of their names quickly.
>
> On the first day of classes, Hernando gives each student a rectangular piece of tag board paper and markers. He asks the students to make "name tents" (paper folded to resemble pup tents). In addition to including their names, Hernando also asks students to decorate the tents to represent something about themselves and then bring them back each day and display them on their desks.

*As he conducts his lessons, Hernando is able to look at the nameplates and start to remember student names. In a few days, he finds that he can name about 80 percent of his students and in the process of learning their names, he learns about each student's personality.*

Consider integrating some student names into your lesson. For example, if you are teaching a unit on France, you might say something like, "If Imani were traveling from Paris to Bordeaux, she might take a train. She might see Brittany on the way . . ." Using student names in a lesson will make the content more personal and help keep students on track and paying attention.

Another way to use names is when asking questions or asking for responses. Rather than waiting for students to raise their hands to respond to a question, some teachers will pose a question and then ask a specific student to respond. It may seem like you are putting the student on the spot, but this strategy, in addition to helping you learn names and show that you know each student individually, will also help keep everyone engaged in the lesson since they don't know whom you will call on next. It also allows you to spread the participation evenly so that all students are accountable for learning.

## Communicate Consistently and Clearly

Clear and consistent communication helps establish and maintain a safe and productive learning environment. If you provide confusing directions or your standards keep changing, it's hard for students to determine the predictability of the learning environment. Before giving directions, it's important to think through what you want from students, and then follow through to make sure students understand and accomplish the task.

Use the following steps to communicate directions consistently and clearly (Eller, 2004).

1. Identify the directions you will need to deliver to students and write them down, particularly if the instructions are complex or involve multiple steps.

2. Break directions down into the subskills that students will need to accomplish for successful completion of the activity, taking the proper order of subskills into consideration.

3. Identify the specific information that the team members will need to be given in order to successfully complete each subskill.

4. Recombine the subskills into their original form, and put the directions in the order they need to be given to ensure successful completion of the entire activity.

5. Walk through the directions, taking note of any areas that could be confusing or hard to follow. Minimize the number of directions you deliver. Write down the steps and the language you will use in delivering the directions to the students.

6. Identify the ways you will check if students understand the directions, and identify alternate ways you can clarify the directions if students are misunderstanding.

7. Jot down in your lesson plan when you will deliver directions and an outline of your plan to deliver them.

Here's an example of how a new teacher, Mable, communicates directions clearly and consistently.

> Mable, a middle school life science teacher, notices that her students have trouble getting started when she assigns them work at their lab stations. She decides that it might be helpful if she looks at how she provides directions. As she thinks about her expectations, she identifies the following steps students will need in order to move from their desks to the lab area and get started on their work:
>
> 1. Students need to review the lab assignment on the board.
> 2. Students need to get a pen and their lab book from their desk.
> 3. Students should push in their chairs and walk over to their lab station.
> 4. Once students are at their lab station, they need to open their lab books and identify the materials needed to complete the lab.
> 5. Once students identify the needed materials, they should take these materials from their lab drawer and place them on the lab countertop.
> 6. After securing the needed materials, students should review the rest of the lab procedures and start following the directions in the lab manual.
> 7. After reading the lab directions, if the students have any questions, they should post their question flag (a flag used in the classroom for students to signal to their teacher that they have a question). The student should wait until the teacher is able to come over to answer their question.
>
> After generating this list of tasks, Mable can see why the students are having trouble at their lab stations: they are not checking their lab manuals to see what supplies they need for the lab. Mable

*decides to use her list of tasks to create new directions for the lab work for students.*

*Before the next lab, Mable conveys the previously mentioned directions to her students. As students review the directions in pairs, Mable walks around the room and listens to their conversations to make sure they understand what to do when she asks them to move to their lab stations.*

As you can see from these steps, it's important to carefully think through what you want students to do, then put those tasks in the proper order. Another important aspect to consider is making sure students understand what you want them to do before you send them off to work on the task. By checking their understanding, you ensure that the product will be what you are looking for in the end. Figure 3.1 (page 68) shows a planning template to help you as you get ready to give students directions.

## Use Appropriate Humor

Using appropriate humor is another way that teachers can develop good relationships with their students. Always keep the term *appropriate* in mind as you consider using humor with your students. Never make a student the topic or target of the humor. Students might appear to be okay with this from the outside, but inside, they might take the humor as negative and a put-down. You could actually damage your reputation with the student or lose his or her trust if you use humor inappropriately.

Avoid sarcasm—humor that involves mocking or ridicule or shows contempt. It may appear that students are laughing along, but in reality, they could be taking offense to your sarcasm. At times, teachers of middle and high school learners try to justify the use of sarcasm on the basis that the students like it, understand it, or are motivated by it. Keep in mind that even though students seem to laugh or be okay with sarcasm, it is not an appropriate form of humor to use with students.

On the other hand, students do like teachers who can laugh at themselves, relate to funny stories, and see the humor in life. A sense of humor shows that you are human and able to laugh at life and at school. Telling funny stories, using appropriate cartoons, and integrating other forms of humor into lessons, the school day, and so on can be motivational for students.

Let's see how one teacher, Marcus, uses humor to handle a situation in his classroom.

1. Identify the directions you will need to deliver to students and write them down, particularly if the instructions are complex or involve multiple steps.

2. Break directions down into the subskills that students will need to accomplish for successful completion of the activity, taking the proper order of subskills into consideration.

3. Identify the specific information that students will need to be given in order to successfully complete each subskill.

4. Recombine the subskills into their original form and put the directions in the order they need to be given to ensure successful completion of the entire activity.

5. Walk through the directions, taking note of any areas that could be confusing or hard to follow. Minimize the number of directions you deliver. Identify how you will deliver the directions to students.

6. Identify the ways you will check if students understand the directions, and identify alternate ways you can clarify the directions if students are misunderstanding.

7. Jot down in your lesson plan when you will deliver directions and an outline of your plan to deliver them.

*Source: Adapted from Eller, 2004.*

Figure 3.1: Direction-planning template.

*Visit **go.solution-tree.com/instruction** to download a free reproducible version of this figure.*

> *Marcus, a junior high Earth science teacher, has to step into the hall just outside his classroom door for a moment to talk to an office staff member. While his back is turned, one of his students pushes the plastic skeleton from the front of the room over to the white board and places a marker in its hand so it appears the skeleton is presenting a lecture.*
>
> *When Marcus comes back into the room, he notices the skeleton and chuckles to himself. Then he walks over to one of the open desks in the front and sits down as if he were a student taking the class. After about ten seconds, he starts to look around, then laugh. He stands up and says, "Is that how I look?" He walks over and moves the skeleton to the side and says, "It doesn't look like the skeleton has a lot to say about today's topic. I should take over the lesson." The students smile and laugh, but then they get back to task once Marcus starts the lesson.*

Not every teacher could think as fast on his or her feet as Marcus did to embrace the humor in a situation. Marcus based the humor on himself, not on one of his students. Marcus also knew how to get the students back on track after using humor. As a result of his use of appropriate humor, Marcus showed his students that he is human and they could relate to him.

## Set Goals With Students

Working with students to set learning goals is a critical activity that will help you communicate expectations to them, get to know them, and build your relationships with them—not to mention, you get to know what their ambitions are for the upcoming school year. Goal setting is also helpful in developing student accountability as the year progresses. When students set their own goals, there is a good chance that both student achievement and student commitment to learning will increase (Stiggins & Chappuis, 2006).

When working with smaller groups or in a self-contained classroom, like at the elementary level, you may be able to work personally with students to help them with the goal-setting process. In larger classrooms and in secondary schools, you may want to model the process and have the students work independently to submit written goals. However you conduct your goal-setting process, there are some important considerations to keep in mind.

▶ Goals need to be attainable for students.

▶ It is best for students to write and monitor their goals so they have ownership.

▶ Goals should be shared with parents.

Working with students to set and reach goals can be rewarding and is crucial for helping them achieve success in your classroom. Carefully think through the process before starting. Figure 3.2 provides some questions for you to use in thinking through how you can use goals and the process of goal setting with students.

---

- What type of system will your students use to develop and maintain their goals?
- How will you support your students in setting and attaining their individual goals?
- How will you keep track of and monitor the students' goals?
- What strategies or actions will you need to put in place for students to meet their goals?
- How will you involve the parents and guardians in the student goal-setting process?
- How will you use parent-teacher conferences as a vehicle to communicate student goals?
- How are student-led conferences a vehicle for students to share their goals?
- How is a portfolio a tool to help students monitor their goals?
- How will students share their goals with you and their parents and guardians?
- What will be the process and time lines for students to monitor their goals?

---

Figure 3.2: Questions to help new teachers think through the goal-setting process.

*Visit go.solution-tree.com/instruction to download a free reproducible version of this figure.*

Student goal setting for learning allows students to set learning targets and then develop strategies to reach their goals. The self-assessment process allows students to monitor and evaluate their performance during a lesson or unit of instruction.

## Setting Goals

Students need help setting personal and learning goals. Providing them with assistance will ensure that goals are achievable and that students can monitor their progress. It also helps you as their new teacher get to know them and their abilities. As a new teacher, you may wonder how you can do this. Figure 3.3 shows a step-by-step process you can share with your students to help them set goals.

---

**Directions:** Use these eight steps to help you as you work to reach the goals you have set for yourself this school year.

1. Identify what your goal will be by using current data and work samples.

2. Write a clear, specific, measurable, attainable, and realistic goal.

3. Design an action plan for each goal.

4. Create a time line for obtaining your goal.

5. Share your goal with your teacher, family member, or someone who will help you obtain your goal.

6. Define the resources you will need to achieve your goal.

7. Reflection is a key component to reaching your goal. Reflect on your goal at least once a week to see if you are on target to completing your goals.

8. Celebrate your success for obtaining your goal!

---

Figure 3.3: Eight steps for student goal setting.

*Visit **go.solution-tree.com/instruction** to download a free reproducible version of this figure.*

You might consider implementing some of these steps individually with your students or in a large-group setting. The more support you can give your students in attaining these goals, the more successful they will be.

Some steps will need to be simplified depending on the age group you teach. Younger students can complete a shorter form, such as the one in figure 3.4, to help them identify and reach their learning goals.

---

**Directions:** Plan your goal, show how you will reach your goal, reflect on your goal, and make a time line to meet your goal. This equals success!

**Name:** Oliver    **Grade:** 8

**My reading or mathematics goal for the year is:** I want to improve my reading ability so I can read harder books.

> **I can reach my goal by:** I can study more and harder vocabulary words. I can check out books at a higher reading level from the library. I'll work with my language arts teacher to talk about what I'm reading and understand what I'm reading.
>
> **My teacher can help me reach my goal by:** She can help me identify more vocabulary words. She can help me find more difficult books that I can read.
>
> **My family can help me reach my goal by:** They can encourage me and ask me how I'm doing on my goals. They can let me know when I'm doing a good job. They can provide a good place for me to read.
>
> **Student signature:** _Oliver Johnson_    **Family member signature:** _Mike Johnson_
>
> **Teacher signature:** _Mrs. Stein_

Figure 3.4: Goal-setting form.

*Visit **go.solution-tree.com/instruction** to download a free reproducible blank template of this figure.*

## Monitoring Student Goals

It is important for you to decide how you are going to monitor students' goals and help them monitor their goals. Take an active role in the process of supporting students as they work to attain their goals. Most students have very little experience setting and following through on school-based goals, so you'll want to help them with the task. It's a good idea to schedule periodic follow-up conferences with your students to see how they're doing in relation to implementing their goals. Some teachers place a reminder in their calendar to periodically meet with students for this follow-up. Figure 3.5 (page 72) is a reflection form to provide guidance for conducting these periodic check-in meetings.

The specific goals students set are up to you and them. Year-long goals should be based on extended learning opportunities or improvements that may take most of the school year to attain. Some examples could include:

- Improving study skills
- Increasing reading speed or comprehension
- Growing in leadership skills
- Improving grades to make the honor role
- Scoring proficient in all areas of the state assessments
- Improving achievement to score at least a twenty-one on the ACT exam
- Improving organizational skills
- Being able to use technology resources to help learning

This school year, you have had the opportunity to set goals for yourself. I am interested in making sure you have a chance to be successful in this process. You and I will periodically meet to review your goal and your progress on your goal.

**Directions:** Please complete the reflection before our scheduled meeting to let me know how things are going in relation to your goal.

**November:** How are you doing on your goal? Please be specific and share what you have or have not accomplished since you set the goal.

**January:** How are you doing on your goal? Please be specific and share what you have or have not accomplished since you set the goal.

**March:** Are you on track for meeting your end-of-the-year goal? Please be specific and share what you have or have not accomplished since you set the goal.

**End of the Year:**

- Did you meet your goal?

- What helped or prevented you from meeting your goal?

- What will you do to continue to work on your goal?

Figure 3.5: Reflection form for periodic goal progress meetings.

*Visit **go.solution-tree.com/instruction** to download a free reproducible version of this figure.*

Even though setting and monitoring long-term goals is important, meeting on a shorter term basis to review the progress on these goals might be helpful to your students. Figure 3.6 is a template you can use for these more frequent goal review sessions.

**Directions:** Use this template to help guide your meetings with students to regularly discuss their progress related to their long-term goals.

**Name:** _____

**Beginning date of goal development:** _____

**Long-term goal statement:**

_____

_____

_____

**GOAL MEETING I**

**Date of meeting:** _____

**Progress made toward goal:**

_____

_____

**Changes needed for original goal:**

_____

_____

**Additional resources and support needed:**

_____

_____

```
┌──────────────────────────────────────────────────────────────────┐
│ GOAL MEETING II                                                    │
│ Date of meeting: _____ │
│ Progress made toward goal:                                         │
│ _____ │
│ _____ │
│ Changes needed for original goal:                                  │
│ _____ │
│ _____ │
│ Additional resources and support needed:                           │
│ _____ │
│ _____ │
├──────────────────────────────────────────────────────────────────┤
│ GOAL MEETING III                                                   │
│ Date of meeting: _____ │
│ Progress made toward goal:                                         │
│ _____ │
│ _____ │
│ Changes needed for original goal:                                  │
│ _____ │
│ _____ │
│ Additional resources and support needed:                           │
│ _____ │
│ _____ │
└──────────────────────────────────────────────────────────────────┘
```

Figure 3.6: Periodic goal review meeting template.

*Visit **go.solution-tree.com/instruction** to download a free reproducible version of this figure.*

## Sharing Goals and Progress

Parent-teacher conferences, student-led conferences, and other parent-teacher communications are great ways for students to share their goals with their parents or guardians and for you to continue to build your relationships with students and their families.

A student-led conference is a time for students to present their learning to their parents or guardians and an opportunity for students to formally reflect on their learning and their goals. Students prepare for the conference by reflecting on their learning and assessing their goals.

In addition to talking about their goals, students can present evidence of their progress related to these goals. Students can present evidence and artifacts—usually in a portfolio—that they have been working on throughout a unit or the school year. The student, with teacher guidance, is the one who selects the work to include in the portfolio. Artifacts should clearly illustrate the student's progress in relation to his or her goals.

For the conference to be successful, you should make sure students understand the purpose of the portfolio.

- It represents some but not all the work they have done in class over a period of time.

- It demonstrates both strengths and weaknesses.

- It will be used to help them reflect on what they have learned and what they still need to learn.

- It will help them to state clear goals for future learning, based on the areas where they need to make more progress. (Assessment for Learning, n.d.b)

In addition to a portfolio, students can keep track of their progress using a folder, a journal, PowerPoint slides, a personal website, or a variety of other technology resources. You and your students are only restricted by your imagination.

Once you have selected the type of system your students will be using to keep track of their work, steer them through the conference process by guiding students and asking them specific questions about their learning and goals.

## Sharing Student Growth

Once students have set goals and started to keep track of their progress toward these goals, it's a good idea to ask them to share their progress with their parents and guardians. A technique that works well for this sharing is a student-led conference. Entire books have been devoted to the topic of student-led conferencing. In this book, we will only touch on some general techniques.

A *student-led conference* is a conference session the student facilitates. In student-led conferencing, the student is in charge of sharing information related to his or her achievement and growth about the determined goals.

Since students may not have had much experience in the past conducting their own conferences, it's a good idea to help them get prepared for the experience.

Figure 3.7 provides a set of questions you can use to guide students as they prepare for student-led conferencing.

Once you have assisted students in planning what information they want to share in a student-led conference, you must then help them plan how they will deliver the information to parents or family members. Conducting a conference may be difficult for students to do on their own, so we suggest you provide a template that will help them plan exactly what they will say.

- What have you learned during this period in relation to your goals? Be sure to also focus on your growth in core academic subjects like reading, mathematics, language arts, and so on.
- What did you find easy about learning to _____?
- What was difficult for you to learn _____ and why?
- What do you find is the best way to learn _____?
- What helped you learn something new? _____
- Have you met your learning goal? _____
- What is your time line to meet your goal? _____

Figure 3.7: Questions to help prepare students for student-led conferences.

*Visit* **go.solution-tree.com/instruction** *to download a free reproducible version of this figure.*

Figure 3.8 provides a template to help students plan what they will say during their student-led conference.

**Directions:** During your student-led conference, you will be following an agenda. For each of the following agenda items, write a script of what you will say during your student-led conference.

**Welcome**

How will you welcome your family members to the conference and thank them for coming?

_____

_____

**Overview of the Conference**

How will you let your parents know what you will be presenting during your conference?

_____

_____

Share your academic progress or your progress on your goals. How will you let your parent know how you're doing at this time in relation to school subjects or your goals?

_____

_____

What do you plan to work on in the future? How will you let your family members know how you plan to improve or keep moving forward with your growth or goals?

_____

_____

What questions do your parents have about what you shared in the conference?

_____

_____

Figure 3.8: Student-led conference script planning template.

*Visit* **go.solution-tree.com/instruction** *to download a free reproducible version of this figure.*

The information in the template in figure 3.8 may seem pretty simple, but keep in mind that leading a conference is something entirely new for students. They may be nervous presenting information about themselves and their academic progress and goals to their parents. You should make sure that the process is clear and straightforward so students feel successful.

## Summary and Reflection

In this chapter, we provided specific strategies for building positive relationships with your students. As you reflect on the major learning in this chapter, please respond to the following questions.

▸ Why is it important to build a positive relationship with students? Why is this important to your future success as a teacher?

▸ How does your communication style with students show your attitude toward them? How can your communication style support or hinder your success?

▸ How can you work with students to understand and reach their goals? How will this help you build your relationship with them?

In the next chapter, we examine building relationships with your students in terms of classroom management. The structure you build in your classroom in the first weeks of school will help you continue your successful journey throughout the year.

# chapter 4

# Developing Processes and Procedures for Classroom Management

*Ghadah, a new middle school teacher, is a bit nervous as she receives her first performance evaluation from her principal. But there is nothing to worry about. Her principal points out how Ghadah has done a good job managing her classes. He shares how well-behaved and on task students are in her classroom. He also discusses how much work Ghadah has put into making her classroom a true learning community and a productive learning atmosphere.*

*After the conference, Ghadah reflects on what she has done to develop such a positive learning environment. At the beginning of the year, she thoroughly explains the processes and procedures students will need to know in order to be successful. She also involves the students in generating their vision for a successful, positive classroom climate. Ghadah reviews basic procedures and classroom rules and expectations. All of her hard work pays off in her ability to create a positive learning atmosphere, and her principal recognizes her efforts.*

Classroom management is one of the core skills new teachers need to master in order to be successful and maintain a productive learning environment, and it is a skill that can be challenging for some. If handled properly, it can help establish credibility and foster a positive relationship among students and between teacher and students. Ghadah utilized some basic classroom-management principles to establish and maintain a productive learning environment. Not only did she share her expectations with students, but she also involved students in helping define their learning needs. The result was a very positive and productive classroom environment.

In this chapter, we will focus on some of the core elements necessary for effective classroom management.

## Building a Positive Classroom Community and Climate

Successful classroom management begins with your ability as the teacher to build a positive community and climate in the classroom. Even though these two concepts are slightly different, they are related. Let's take a look at each concept in greater detail.

### Community

When we refer to a classroom *community*, we are talking about a classroom in which there is a strong positive connection among students and between students and the teacher. A classroom community is a group that works together toward common goals and where each person is valued and there is a respect for diverse ways of thinking. In classrooms where the concept of community has been established, everyone has a common connection and an investment in the group's success.

### Climate

The classroom's *climate* is the emotional feel of the space. Successful classroom management is based on the establishment of a positive classroom climate. A positive classroom climate includes a feeling of safety, a sense of being welcome, the feeling that the teacher likes each student and wants all to be successful, and a respect for the differences each student brings to the learning environment.

### Strategies for Building Community and Climate

As a thriving new teacher, you must incorporate strategies into your classroom to develop a sense of community and a positive climate. If the climate is positive, you will be providing a safe atmosphere where students can learn. A classroom community is an environment in which students from varying backgrounds and with different abilities can work together for the common good. Climate and community provide the foundation for your work in classroom management.

#### Collaborative Defining of Classroom Expectations

Asking students to collaborate on defining and determining classroom expectations is a good way to get them engaged in and committed to the expectations and develop a sense of classroom community. This happens because when they collaborate to develop expectations, students are working together to define what they think is important in a positive classroom climate. You can hold informal discussions about expectations or develop a more formal process to identify parameters. Some teachers find the activity in figure 4.1 helpful in leading this discussion.

- Share with students the importance of having their input in developing the behavioral and learning expectations for the classroom.
- Divide the class into smaller groups of two or three students.
- Give each group a sheet of paper with the following questions.
  - What behaviors do we expect from ourselves as learners in this classroom?
  - What behaviors do we expect from each other as learners in this classroom?
  - What do we expect from our teacher in order to help us as learners in this classroom?
- Have them report on their work once all the groups have completed their lists.
- Write down the main expectations generated in the three categories on the board or a piece of chart paper.
- Once all of the groups have reported on their lists, sum them up and add anything you feel is important that the group may have missed.
- Hold a discussion with students after the final list is written to get their commitment to the expectations.

*Source: Adapted from Eller & Eller, 2009.*

Figure 4.1: Our classroom expectations activity.

The activity figure 4.1 outlines is probably best suited for students in the upper elementary grades through high school. In order to use it with younger students, a teacher may choose to hold a discussion with students about behavior expectations for the class. As the students share ideas, you may need to write them down. When working with younger students, limit their expectation list to a small number (three or four expectations). If the list gets too long, it may be harder for students to remember all the expectations.

The expectations students generate for their classroom will vary. Some typical expectations include the following.

▶ Young students (preschool to grade 3)

- Listen to each other.
- Be nice to each other.
- Do our best in school.

▶ Intermediate students (grades 4 to 7)

- Everyone should respect each other and their opinions.
- Complete and turn in your assignments on time.

- Don't put anyone down in class.
- No one else talks when the teacher is presenting information or answering questions.
- Everyone respect each other's property.

▶ Older students (grades 8 to 12)

- The classroom should be an environment where everyone feels safe to share their opinions, learn, and try.
- When students are working together as a team on a project, everyone should do their share of the work.
- When someone is talking, others should show respect by listening and not sharing their opinions until that person is finished.
- No one person should dominate a conversation. Everyone should be able to share their ideas and opinions.
- Students in this classroom should show respect for each other.

### Classroom Covenant

Another activity that helps students develop a sense of community and a positive climate in relation to expectations and rules is a classroom covenant. A *classroom covenant* is a binding agreement about expectations in the classroom. The term *covenant* evokes a stronger emotional commitment than an agreement. By using this stronger term, you are communicating the agreement's importance. When establishing a classroom covenant, it's important to engage all students in the initial conversation about expectations, then work to get everyone's commitment. The concept of a classroom covenant works best in a classroom where the teacher spends a significant amount of time with students. It is less effective in a situation where students move to a number of classrooms throughout the day, such as a typical high school setting.

Figure 4.2 provides a process for developing a classroom covenant.

A classroom covenant can take many forms based on the personalities of the teacher and the students in the class. Figure 4.3 shows a sample covenant.

In the sample, note that the guidelines are very general and represent a big-picture view of the classroom guidelines. After you draft the covenant, ask everyone in the learning community to sign it.

1. Hold an open conversation in the classroom about acceptable classroom behaviors and what students need to see and feel in the classroom so they can concentrate and learn. Ask the students to state their expectations as dos rather than don'ts. (For example, "Listen as others are sharing their ideas" rather than "Don't interrupt while others are talking.")

2. Once the group has had this initial conversation, write the major needs on a piece of chart paper. Then add the title "Classroom Covenant" at the top of the paper.

3. Once all of the expectations are written on the chart paper, review them to make sure they are clear. Then ask if there are any expectations students don't feel they can follow. If there are, clarify what aspect the student may not be able to follow. The expectation could be changed, or you might help the students see how they can follow the existing expectation.

4. After clarifying the expectations, post the classroom covenant in the front of the room and ask each student to sign it and agree to follow it.

5. Periodically, remind students about the covenant and the expectations.

Figure 4.2: Steps for establishing a classroom covenant.

---

**Ms. Smith's Class Covenant**

We believe that we need to work together for the common good of all students in our learning community. In order for this to happen, we need a set of guidelines we can all follow. The following classroom covenant is that set of guidelines.

In Ms. Smith's learning community, we agree to:

- Respect each other and our unique ideas and abilities.
- Openly discuss issues as a group. Use everyone's thoughts in developing solutions to the issues we face.
- Listen as others talk and try to understand what they are saying.
- Use group consensus to make decisions.
- Try hard to do our best in our work at school. Help each other be successful.

Continue to grow and learn together as a classroom community.

Figure 4.3: Sample classroom covenant.

By involving students in generating at least some classroom expectations, you will get more buy-in and commitment from them. Also, when there is a violation, you can focus on the fact that students agreed to the expectations as they were established by everyone. This makes it harder for a student to claim that he or she did not understand an expectation, and it helps you remind the student of the expectation and move forward in a positive manner.

## Establishing Rules

It is best to work together with students to establish expectations for appropriate behavior, but it is necessary to have some non-negotiable rules to successfully operate your classroom. When you present these rules to students, be sure to include your reasoning. Helping students understand why rules are important is essential to achieving their buy in. Keep the following ideas in mind as you develop non-negotiable rules for your classroom.

▸ **Keep your list of rules short:** This helps students keep track of them and prevents the appearance that you have an unending and overwhelming list of expectations.

▸ **Design rules that are broad in scope:** By having a few rules that cover a broader range of behaviors, you'll cover more issues while appearing to have a shorter list of expectations. Also, broader rules can be interpreted to deal with a wider range of behaviors. For example, a rule like, "Keep your hands, feet, and other objects to yourself" covers a lot of ground.

▸ **Make sure your rules address major issues and are not focused on common sense or issues that can be interpreted as petty:** For example, a rule to address the issue of cheating could be stated as, "No cheating is allowed" without listing all of the possible ways that students might think of to cheat. In presenting the rule, a teacher might consider talking about some of the details to ensure student understanding. By listing only the general rule category, a teacher avoids listing minute details that make the rule list sound petty or too detailed.

▸ **Write the rules so the focus is more on doing the positive and less focused on prohibiting a behavior:** For example, the rule that is stated as, "Don't come to class late" would be better stated as "Be in your seat and ready to learn at the start of class." Students may try to defy prohibitive rules. Stating the rule as a positive behavior expectation may help them stay on track.

▸ **Include a catchall rule at the end of your list in case you have forgotten anything:** For example, "Respect the rights and feelings of others" can be applied to almost any behavioral situation to help maintain a positive learning environment and a sense of community.

If done in a positive and proactive manner in which you explain your reasoning and rationale, students are likely to buy in to the expectations and follow the rules.

## Establishing Processes and Procedures

Helping students successfully follow the procedures and processes of your classroom is necessary if you are to create a positive and productive learning community and climate. Within every classroom there are a core set of procedures and processes that students must follow. Establish the routines associated with these procedures and processes during your first weeks of school when students are learning what to expect from you. Think about how you will teach students the proper processes for signaling for attention, speaking in class and using appropriate voice levels, entering and leaving the classroom without disturbing others, turning in completed work, and other essential procedures for success in your class. As a new teacher, you can't assume your students will come with these skills or remember them from last year.

Obviously, how you teach the core set of procedures and processes will depend on the grade level you instruct, student maturity, and so on. If you are teaching at the high school level, you'll probably involve students in a discussion. If you are teaching elementary grades, you may break the procedures into small parts and teach a new part each day. If you are a middle school or junior high teacher, you may pick a core set of behaviors and discuss some while having the students generate a list of others.

### Determine Your Essentials

Before you teach students about the procedures, processes, and rules needed for success in your learning environment, you have to identify them for yourself. Depending on your teaching style, the content area you teach, any safety issues in your classroom (such as equipment or conditions, number of students leaving and entering the classroom, items students need to bring or take with them, and so on), your tolerance for noise, and other factors, you'll want to think about the processes and procedures that will make your classroom a productive learning environment.

Your teaching methods—how you present information, how students process it, and how they demonstrate it—in large part determine what procedures and processes will be essential for your students to learn and for you to manage in the classroom. While many teachers use a variety of teaching methods depending on the situation, activity, student needs, and so on, you will find that you may have a preference for a particular style. Figure 4.4 (page 84) contains an activity for identifying your preferred teaching style and the subsequent behaviors that are necessary to cultivate in your students.

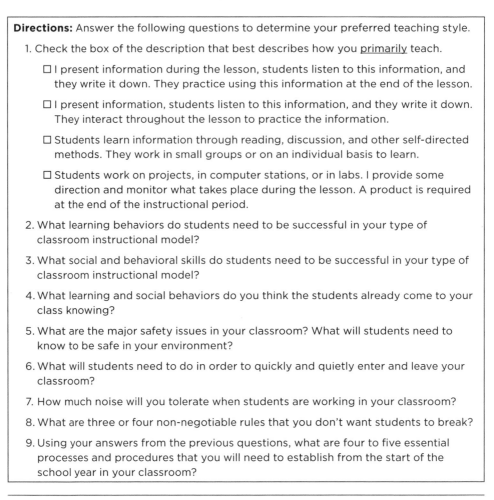

**Directions:** Answer the following questions to determine your preferred teaching style.

1. Check the box of the description that best describes how you <u>primarily</u> teach.

    ☐ I present information during the lesson, students listen to this information, and they write it down. They practice using this information at the end of the lesson.

    ☐ I present information, students listen to this information, and they write it down. They interact throughout the lesson to practice the information.

    ☐ Students learn information through reading, discussion, and other self-directed methods. They work in small groups or on an individual basis to learn.

    ☐ Students work on projects, in computer stations, or in labs. I provide some direction and monitor what takes place during the lesson. A product is required at the end of the instructional period.

2. What learning behaviors do students need to be successful in your type of classroom instructional model?

3. What social and behavioral skills do students need to be successful in your type of classroom instructional model?

4. What learning and social behaviors do you think the students already come to your class knowing?

5. What are the major safety issues in your classroom? What will students need to know to be safe in your environment?

6. What will students need to do in order to quickly and quietly enter and leave your classroom?

7. How much noise will you tolerate when students are working in your classroom?

8. What are three or four non-negotiable rules that you don't want students to break?

9. Using your answers from the previous questions, what are four to five essential processes and procedures that you will need to establish from the start of the school year in your classroom?

Figure 4.4: Template for determining your preferred teaching style and the subsequent behaviors to cultivate in your students.

*Visit* **go.solution-tree.com/instruction** *to download a free reproducible version of this figure.*

Once you've completed the template in figure 4.4, you can use the information from your responses to decide what skills are essential in your classroom for student success. For example, if the major learning mode you use is project completion, then your students will need to be able to work on their own with little teacher direction. If the primary learning mode in your classroom is listening and discussion, then the students will need to be able to pay attention, take notes, and talk in quiet voices during discussions.

Identifying a core set of student behavior skills is essential for student success. Some teachers find value in operating classrooms where they don't have to direct every learning activity. In this type of classroom, students need to build their skills in performing tasks without teacher direction. The following list (figure 4.5) shows a set of skills that you may find helpful if you are operating your classroom in this way. These skills not only help students work without teacher direction, they also help to contribute to a well-managed classroom. For example, one of the skills requires students to stop what they are doing and look at the teacher when they hear the agreed-on signal for attention. Mastering this skill helps with classroom management because all the teacher has to do is state the key phrase (the signal) and students will stop what they are doing and listen. Without this skill, a teacher may need to spend a lot of time, raise his or her voice, and use other strategies to get everyone to stop and listen at the same time. Using a signal saves time and promotes an orderly classroom environment. Figure 4.5 is a checklist you can use to determine the self-management skills you want to focus on in your classroom.

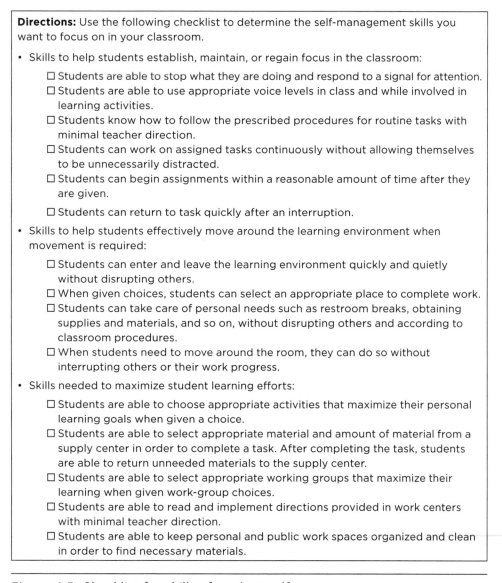

**Directions:** Use the following checklist to determine the self-management skills you want to focus on in your classroom.

- Skills to help students establish, maintain, or regain focus in the classroom:
    - ☐ Students are able to stop what they are doing and respond to a signal for attention.
    - ☐ Students are able to use appropriate voice levels in class and while involved in learning activities.
    - ☐ Students know how to follow the prescribed procedures for routine tasks with minimal teacher direction.
    - ☐ Students can work on assigned tasks continuously without allowing themselves to be unnecessarily distracted.
    - ☐ Students can begin assignments within a reasonable amount of time after they are given.
    - ☐ Students can return to task quickly after an interruption.
- Skills to help students effectively move around the learning environment when movement is required:
    - ☐ Students can enter and leave the learning environment quickly and quietly without disrupting others.
    - ☐ When given choices, students can select an appropriate place to complete work.
    - ☐ Students can take care of personal needs such as restroom breaks, obtaining supplies and materials, and so on, without disrupting others and according to classroom procedures.
    - ☐ When students need to move around the room, they can do so without interrupting others or their work progress.
- Skills needed to maximize student learning efforts:
    - ☐ Students are able to choose appropriate activities that maximize their personal learning goals when given a choice.
    - ☐ Students are able to select appropriate material and amount of material from a supply center in order to complete a task. After completing the task, students are able to return unneeded materials to the supply center.
    - ☐ Students are able to select appropriate working groups that maximize their learning when given work-group choices.
    - ☐ Students are able to read and implement directions provided in work centers with minimal teacher direction.
    - ☐ Students are able to keep personal and public work spaces organized and clean in order to find necessary materials.

Figure 4.5: Checklist for skills of student self-management.

*Visit **go.solution-tree.com/instruction** to download a free reproducible version of this figure.*

As you can see, the skills of student independence focus on several crucial areas of classroom operation. Some of these areas are important in classrooms where students are involved in centers, labs, and other small-group activities, while others are important in almost any other classroom setting. As a new teacher, you will want to determine which skills are most essential for your classroom setting.

## Teach the Essentials

Once you have determined the essential processes and procedures needed for success in your classroom, you will need to develop lessons to teach students these essentials. Start by developing a schedule to introduce a small set of procedures each day during the first two weeks of school that includes when the behaviors will be taught, when they will be practiced, and when they will be reinforced.

Figure 4.6 provides a comprehensive two-week example for new teachers to teach and track the skills of student self-management. The example has been primarily designed for implementation for students in grades 2 to 10. In implementing it in your specific setting, you may want to change how you present the behavior expectations and skill descriptions to students and how they practice these new skills. For example, some older students may think it's silly to practice using various voice-volume levels after you tell them about your expectations. Some teachers give students a choice by saying, "I've explained my expectations for the various voice-volume levels I want you to use during small-group work. Can you use these in the future, or do you think we need to practice them?" By providing the students with the choice, you communicate that you are confident in their level of maturity. If later they are unable to demonstrate the expected skill, you may need to ask them to practice it.

The example in figure 4.6 shows how the teacher has included periodic and repeated opportunities to practice the skills he or she has introduced to the students.

## Practice the Essentials

Students' ability to learn and internalize the processes and procedures of self-management depends on two elements of effective practice: scheduling the practice and reinforcing behavior.

### Scheduling the Practice

Scheduling the practice is essential to the success of students learning these skills. There are three aspects of practice you'll want to think about:

**Directions:** Use this form to map out how you plan to teach, practice, and reinforce new skills of student self-management in your classroom. List the behaviors you are tracking and the reinforcers you are planning to use.

| Behaviors You Plan to Practice | Reinforcers You Plan to Use |
|---|---|
| • Signaling for attention<br>• Coming into class without disrupting other students<br>• Using proper voice-volume levels in the classroom<br>• Getting needed materials for work<br>• Moving around the room<br>• Returning to task quickly after an interruption | • Verbal praise<br>• Class rewards |

| | Monday | Tuesday | Wednesday | Thursday | Friday |
|---|---|---|---|---|---|
| **Week 1** | Teach signal, 9 a.m.<br><br>Practice signal, 10 a.m.<br><br>Practice signal, 1 p.m. | Practice signal, 9 a.m.<br><br>Practice signal, 11 a.m.<br><br>Practice signal, 1 p.m. | Practice signal, 8:55 a.m.<br><br>Teach coming into class, 9 a.m.<br><br>Practice coming into class, 10:30 a.m.<br><br>Practice signal, 11:00 a.m.<br><br>Practice coming into class, 11:30 a.m. | Use signal throughout the day to get student attention.<br><br>Teach voice levels, 9:00 a.m.<br><br>Practice coming into class, 10:00 a.m.<br><br>Practice voice levels, 11:00 a.m.<br><br>Practice voice levels, 1 p.m. | Continue to use signal throughout the day to get student attention.<br><br>Remind students about coming into class properly, and praise them when they do so.<br><br>Teach students to get materials, 9 a.m.; practice voice levels. |
| **Week 2** | Review the previous week's skills, and remind students about the expectations, 9 a.m.<br><br>Introduce moving around the room without disturbing others, 10 a.m.<br><br>Practice moving around the room, 1 p.m.<br><br>Practice signal throughout the day. | Practice signal, 9 a.m.<br><br>Practice moving around the room, 10:30 a.m.<br><br>Practice getting needed materials, 1 p.m.<br><br>Practice voice levels, 2 p.m. | Introduce returning to class quickly after an interruption, 9 a.m.<br><br>Practice returning to task, 10:30 a.m.<br><br>Practice returning to task, 1:30 p.m.<br><br>Practice signaling for attention throughout the day.<br><br>Practice moving around the room, 2:00 p.m. | Practice all previously taught skills throughout the day. | Practice all previously taught skills throughout the day. |

Figure 4.6: Sample planning template to track learning processes and procedures.

*Visit go.solution-tree.com/instruction to download a free reproducible blank template of this figure.*

(1) massing and (2) distributing the practice and (3) making an academic connection to the skill.

In the initial stages of learning, you should bunch together or mass the practice of the new skills. In *massing the practice*, you provide many opportunities over a short period of time in order to help students learn quickly. After teaching a new process or procedure, some teachers practice the skill five to ten times during the first day.

After the initial learning stages, you should periodically reteach and have students practice the skill. This periodic review is called *distributing the practice*. Distributing the practice allows students to better internalize the concepts since they are going to occasionally review them.

Ensuring that students make the procedures and process part of their daily routines is helping *make an academic connection*. Teachers make this connection by coupling the skills with academic content. For example, in practicing the concept of signaling for attention, you could ask students to practice the skill during an academic lesson. For appropriate voice levels, ask students to practice using appropriate voice levels while involved with a small-group activity within an academic content area. When working with older students who are not necessarily practicing the new behaviors before their use, it will be important for you to give them the opportunity to use the skill as soon as possible after your explanation so it becomes a part of their normal behavior.

The academic connection is something you should include as you plan to develop the skills of procedures and processes in your students.

*Teaching the Practice*

For most student age groups, it's important that you go beyond just telling students about the processes and procedures in your classroom. You'll want to actually teach them these essential items. The best way to do this is to develop lessons to teach processes and procedures just like you do when teaching academic subjects. Following is a lesson design outline illustrating the various components that need to be included in lessons where the teacher is trying to help students learn the skills of student self-management.

1. **Opening or warm-up activity:** To establish a focus for the behavior lesson, it's important to provide a warm-up for the lesson. This activity also helps establish the reasons for the lesson and identifies the behavior skill. It's best to help the students see how the skill or skills will benefit them in your classroom and in their own learning during this step.

2. **Sharing the lesson objective or learning target:** In this part of the lesson, you share its reason or purpose. Also share what your expectations are for student learning and use of the new behavior skill both in the short-term (at the end of the lesson) and long-term (during the course, semester, year, and so on). The lesson objective should be phrased in a manner that students will easily understand.

3. **Helping students learn the critical behaviors:** In this part of the lesson, you help students learn the desired behavior or skills of student self-management. How this process happens is based on the age level of the students and the teacher's instructional preferences. In early elementary classrooms, you may present the information, while middle or high school teachers may draw this information from the students. In other words, engage older students in large- or small-group discussions in which they are asked to share examples where they have seen or used the skills in the past. Asking them for their experiences may help alleviate any thoughts that the conversation is trivial.

4. **Making sure students understand the critical behaviors through demonstration:** Make sure that students can show or demonstrate that they understand the expected behaviors during this part of the lesson. The emphasis here should be on actually having students demonstrate the learning rather than just saying they understand. Paraphrasing the major points, demonstrating the major points, writing the behavioral expectations on paper, talking about the expectations with a partner, and so on are ways students can demonstrate their understanding. Making sure students understand the expectations is crucial in holding them accountable later.

5. **Guiding initial practice of the behaviors:** As students first begin to use the required skill of student self-management, it's important that you guide them through the process. This guidance will ensure that they are correctly practicing the skills. Typically, the teacher provides feedback on the students' efforts during this initial practice session. For most age groups, this practice will give students a chance to use their new skills in a trial situation before they need to apply the knowledge to real situations. You may not require older students to practice the new behaviors during your lesson or explanation. This practice may come later as they are using the skill in a real situation.

6. **Helping students practice the new behaviors on their own:** Eventually, you need to help students use the new skill of student self-management in independent situations. In order to do this, pair a

new behavior skill with an academic activity. This academic activity should be something that is not new learning or extremely difficult for the student to complete. It is also in this phase that you will use both massed and distributed practice and positive reinforcers to make the new behavior skill a habit and ensure independent use of the skill in the classroom.

Figure 4.7 shows a sample completed lesson design for teaching using a signal.

---

1. **Opening or warm-up activity:** *How many of you want to be able to get your work completed plus work with others in groups in the classroom? [Students raise their hands.] In order for that to happen, I need to be able to get your attention when I need to share announcements or provide you with information.*

2. **Sharing the lesson objective:** *Today, we will be learning about a signal that I will use in helping get your attention and focus when I need it. When we finish, you will be able to focus immediately when I provide the signal.*

3. **Helping students learn the critical behaviors:** *The signal for attention will be "I need your attention please." When you hear "I need your attention please," you need to stop what you are doing, look at me, and listen to what I will be telling you next. These are the same behaviors that people need to use when approaching a train crossing (stop, look, and listen).*

4. **Making sure students understand the critical behaviors through demonstration:** *I know these behaviors (stop, look, and listen) are clear, but I want to make sure that I know you understand them. Talk in pairs about what our signal for attention is and what you should do when you hear it. [As students are talking, the teacher walks around and listens to the conversations.]*

5. **Guiding initial practice of the behaviors:** *I can see that all of you know what to do when you hear the signal "I need your attention please." Let's try this out now. I'm going to have you meet in small groups and talk about what you did last weekend. During the conversation, I'll use the signal. When you hear it, stop, look, and listen immediately. Ready? Meet in pairs. Go! [After about three to four seconds of conversation, the teacher uses the signal. After students hear it and act, the teacher gives feedback on their efforts. This cycle is repeated four to five times during the next two or three minutes.]*

6. **Helping students practice the new behaviors on their own:** *Once students have learned the signal, students practice it seven to ten more times during the day. Each day, for the next two weeks, the teacher should purposefully practice the new behavior skills with increasingly more difficult content and in varying situations.*

---

Figure 4.7: Sample lesson design for a skill of independence.

*Visit **go.solution-tree.com/instruction** to download a free reproducible blank template of this figure.*

As you can see in the sample, the teacher who implemented this lesson used a step-by-step process. Each lesson component is designed to assist the students in learning and practicing the new behavior just like a teacher would want them to do if they were learning an academic skill.

### Reinforcing Behavior

*Reinforcement* simply refers to the process where teachers recognize the efforts of students as they exhibit the new or desired behaviors. The following sections highlight some of the basic concepts of reinforcement.

#### Positive Reinforcement

With positive reinforcement, teachers provide students with something the student wants or needs when he or she exhibits a desired behavior. Positive reinforcement is only effective if the person receiving it sees it as desirable. Some examples of positive reinforcers include praise from a significant person, recognition from a teacher, public recognition, positive feedback, and tangible rewards (points, stickers, candy, and so on).

#### Negative Reinforcement

Negative reinforcement involves receiving something that is not wanted or desired. Since the reinforcement is unwanted, students try to remove or end the unwanted reinforcer by stopping or changing the behavior. Negative reinforcement is different than consequences (punishment) because with negative reinforcement, the student can remove the negative reinforcer by changing the behavior. With consequences, no matter what the student does, the punishment is still administered. Examples of negative reinforcers include the teacher standing close to a student (proximity control), asking the student to move to a new seat until he or she decides to pay attention, and stopping a lesson and looking at the student until he or she quiets down.

Negative reinforcement is less effective than positive reinforcement because we can't always predict what behavior the student will exhibit in order to remove the negative reinforcer. The new behavior could be worse and the negative behavior strengthened.

#### Extinction

*Extinction* is when a behavior receives no reinforcement so it eventually diminishes and goes away. In a classroom, you could choose to ignore minor behaviors in the hope that they will go away. Extinction will work if the behavior receives no reinforcement from any source. If other students laugh at the behavior or applaud when the student enacts the behavior, this is reinforcement. As a teacher, you have to eliminate all sources of reinforcement for extinction to work.

Let's see how Gracious, a new teacher, uses reinforcement to help his students learn the skill of using appropriate voice levels in the classroom.

*Gracious, a new fourth-grade teacher, has just completed a lesson with his class related to using appropriate voice levels when they are working in small groups. After the lesson, he assigns students to small groups, provides them with a discussion topic, and then asks them to practice using the "group voice" level he has just taught.*

*Within the first ten seconds of the activity, Gracious notices that two of the groups are using the group voice level in their discussion. He immediately gives the signal for attention to pause the conversation. Once the students are all looking at him he gives positive reinforcement by saying, "I noticed that groups two and six are really doing a great job using our new group voice." He then directs all of the groups to start their conversations again.*

*As he walks around the classroom listening to the conversations, Gracious notices that one of the groups is talking more loudly than they should. He stops, stands by the group, and then gestures for them to lower their voices by holding his hand palm down and moving it toward the floor. The group immediately lowers its voice level due to this negative reinforcement.*

*After several more positive comments, Gracious stops the entire class and thanks them for such a good demonstration of the proper voice levels (positive reinforcement). Gracious says, "I can see that all of you now know how to use the proper voice level when working in a small group. I expect to see you using this voice level whenever we work in small groups."*

In this example, we can see how Gracious noticed as soon as the students exhibited the proper behavior and praised them for their efforts. This reinforcement let them know they were doing exactly what he wanted and that he appreciated their efforts. His quick recognition helped to make their use of the proper voice levels stronger and thus more likely to continue in the future.

## Provide Students With Choices

When working with potentially disruptive students and situations, it's a good practice to provide students with choices. Providing students with choices during difficult classroom situations gives them the opportunity to feel in control of their behavior and turn the situation around. As you think about providing choices, consider the following.

▸ **Make sure you are comfortable providing choices for the particular student or situation:** For example, telling a student, "You can choose a place to work unless you want me to choose one for you" may sound like something good to say, but what will you do if a confrontation ensues over seat selection? It might be better to say, "Please find a seat so we can start class."

▸ **Make sure you are suggesting viable choices:** For example, saying, "You can sit here or join the group on the other side of the room" provides a clear choice. However, saying to a student, "Find a seat or you'll have to suffer the consequences" is less about providing a choice than it is about threatening the student.

▸ **Speak in a calm, relaxed voice:** If you raise your voice, it could escalate a student's negative behavior. Calmly stating to a student, "Please start on your assignment or take a few minutes to review your notes" in a rational voice lets the student know you are under control and not confronting him or her, but rather asking him or her to comply. If you were to move closer to the student and then raise your voice stating, "I said get to work or leave the classroom!" you are starting a confrontation with the student that could be met with resistance.

▸ **Be firm:** Clearly state the choices, and then stop and wait for the student to respond. Don't say, "Okay?" or remind the student right away. Pausing will let the student know that you mean what you say. Sometimes, students have learned to just wait out adults when they are given choices, or, worse yet, they are accustomed to adults lecturing or scolding them but not following through. If you start by making a request but then back down, students will quickly learn that you don't mean what you say.

▸ **Avoid sarcasm or condescending comments:** As stated in the section "Use Appropriate Humor" (page 67), avoid humor that involves mocking or ridicule or shows contempt. It may appear that students are laughing along, but in reality, they could be taking offense to your sarcasm. Instead, encourage students as they make their decisions.

▸ **Allow the student time to consider the choices before making a decision:** You may even want to step away from the situation to allow the student to make a decision. Stepping away lowers the conflict related to the situation and gives the student the opportunity to make a selection while saving face with his or her peers.

▶ **Positively reinforce the student for making a choice, and then move on with the lesson:** When the student makes the choice, you can say, "Thank you (student name). I knew you would make the best choice."

▶ **Consider allowing students to make choices in situations that are not tense or confrontational:** If you show students that this is an important skill by taking the time to help them develop their decision-making skills, they will learn to make good decisions and avoid confrontational situations.

## Determine and Deliver Consequences

The behavior management strategies in this chapter are designed to help you proactively address and minimize potential behavior issues. Preventing or minimizing disruptions will enable you to work with students in a more collaborative manner and build a positive classroom climate and a productive learning community.

Even the most experienced teacher cannot anticipate and prevent every possible behavior issue. So what happens when students do not live up to expectations—when their behavior is out of bounds and they break rules that have been established as part of your classroom community? You may need to provide consequences. When you were in school, teachers may have used consequences as their first tool to shape student behavior. You may find it helpful to implement the other tools in the chapter before using consequences.

Consequences are somewhat like negative reinforcers because they occur as a result of a student action. Consequences are slightly different than negative reinforcers, however, because they are a little harder for the student to remove. The following is an example.

> As her class works in small groups to balance chemical equations, Kim walks around the classroom to monitor the groups. She notices that one of the groups appears to be off task. Kim decides to stand by this group (a negative reinforcement). In response to her proximity, the group gets back on task. A few minutes later, Kim notices that the group is off task and group members are pushing each other. This time, Kim separates the group members and asks them to meet with her after class. During this after-class meeting, Kim asks the group members to talk about why their behavior is not within her expectations. She asks them to generate some ideas about how they can work together in the future and stay on track (a consequence). They also have to determine how they will make up the time they wasted in class and the time Kim spent dealing with the situation.

In this example, we see how Kim first used proximity (a negative reinforcer) to attempt to manage the small group's behavior. When that strategy didn't work, she moved to a consequence (keeping the students after class and asking them to develop a plan to make up the time they wasted) to further shape their behavior. In this case, the consequence was designed to help the students learn from the situation. Consequences have attributes that make them effective.

Keep the following in mind as you think about designing consequences.

▸ **Make sure the consequences are instructional in nature:** For example, asking a student to design a plan to make up for the time wasted by his behavior will help the student learn the impact of his behavior and hopefully avoid it in the future.

▸ **Design consequences that fit the student's infraction:** If the student's behavior is minor, make the consequence minor. If the behavior is more severe, the consequence should be more severe. For example, if a student damages another student's property, the consequence might be to work at the school in order to earn enough to replace the damaged property.

▸ **Select consequences that are simple and straightforward to implement:** By stating the consequence clearly and avoiding lecturing and shaming the student, the consequence will be more effective. For example, clearly stating, "You took five minutes of our learning time today because I had to redirect you. You'll need to make up that time after school" describes the issue. On the other hand, if a teacher said, "You know, you really irritated me. I'm so upset by your childish behavior. You wasted the taxpayers' money today and all of our students are now behind" the student will probably not learn from the consequence.

▸ **Select consequences that maintain the student's dignity:** Avoid lecturing or shaming the student. Delivering the consequence without adding your feelings (or other drama) will help prevent the student feeling attacked. Describing the behavior and not focusing on the person will help you deliver consequences that maintain dignity. For example, saying, "You wasted time in class today as a result of . . ." maintains the student's dignity. Stating, "What's wrong with you? Are you stupid?" does not. Keep your temper under control so you don't fall into this trap.

▸ **Be sure to follow through and implement your stated consequences.** Remember to deliver the consequences fairly and rationally, avoiding an emotional outburst. Also be sure to avoid drawing undo attention to the offending student. If possible, involve the student in a debriefing about what he or she learned as a result of the consequence.

## Summary and Reflection

In this chapter, we explored effective classroom-management strategies you can use as a new teacher. As you reflect on what you've learned, respond to the following questions.

▸ Why is it important to identify your preferred teaching style when considering the processes and procedures you decide to teach your students?

▸ How can teaching the procedures and processes in your classroom contribute to good classroom management?

▸ How might you periodically have students practice their new skills when teaching lessons on the skills of student responsibility?

▸ Think about the role of positive reinforcement. How can you use it to shape behavior? How can you use extinction to extinguish minor behaviors in the classroom?

You have learned some basic information in this chapter to help you get off to a great start with classroom management. Once you have taught skills for student independence, you'll need to have students regularly practice their newly developed skills until they become good habits.

In the next chapter, you will learn strategies to deal with situations in which students have become disruptive and out of control. The strategies will help you keep calm while dealing with these difficult situations.

# chapter 5
# Managing Difficult Behaviors

*Cindy, a new middle-school teacher, has most of her class working productively after she takes time to create a positive classroom climate by teaching students the behaviors she wants them to use in class. She has developed a community of learners within her classroom, and students are working together to solve problems within a positive environment.*

*One day a new student, Debra, transfers to Cindy's classroom. When she arrives, Cindy can see immediately that Debra is exhibiting some challenging behaviors. Even though Cindy's class welcomes Debra, she isn't making friends. She is sometimes disruptive during lessons, causing some of the other students to laugh and make comments. For example, Debra coughs or clears her throat whenever she doesn't like something Cindy says. She also makes comments to herself loud enough so other students can overhear.*

*Cindy can see that Debra is getting attention from other students as a result of her disruptive behaviors. Cindy knows she needs a plan to manage Debra's disruptive behaviors and help her develop more positive behavior.*

Many new teachers struggle with managing difficult behaviors like Debra's. They haven't had as much experience dealing with disruptive behaviors, de-escalating off-task behavior, and developing plans to work individually with students to shape their behavior. The good news is that new teachers can learn the skills required to manage students displaying disruptive or difficult behavior.

Classroom-management strategies are highly contextual and need to be implemented in a manner that fits the climate and the culture of your classroom and school. Though the strategies and best practices in this chapter have been used successfully by many teachers, it is important to keep in mind that you may need to make adjustments or change some of the strategies to fit your unique situation.

## Managing Difficult and Disruptive Students

Teachers who successfully manage difficult and disruptive students possess a core set of skills. These skills enable them to quickly diagnose a disruptive or difficult situation then quickly put in place a strategy to address it. These essential skills include:

- ▸ A clear understanding of the behaviors required to be successful in your classroom. Be sure to think about what you are expecting from your students in order for them to be successful in your classroom.

- ▸ The ability to emotionally disconnect from the problem behavior or issue. When a student exhibits negative behavior, do not take it personally. Instead, react in a calm but firm manner.

- ▸ The ability to observe and accurately describe the problem behavior. Be sure you can identify and explain the exact behavior you observe and want the student to diminish. If you can't tell a student exactly what he or she did that was wrong, it's going to be hard for the student to change his or her behavior.

- ▸ An understanding of the bigger picture and the patience to resolve the problem behavior in a step-by-step manner. A student's problem behavior may be a smaller part of a larger issue. Start by addressing a small part of the situation and know that it may take time to get the student back on track.

- ▸ The ability to design and implement an improvement plan to reduce the disruptive or difficult behavior. Most students with complex behavior issues respond well to a comprehensive plan. Think about how you might develop one to attack the issue.

- ▸ The ability to break desired behavior into small, teachable parts. A student may only be able to manage a small change at first. Focus on small steps when addressing complex issues.

- ▸ The ability to examine all issues impacting a problem behavior— including your own teaching. Keep in mind that you, your classroom structure, your behaviors, and other factors may be contributing to the situation. For example, a student may enter your classroom and on the way to her desk disrupt five students. Maybe the location of her desk is contributing to the problem.

Figure 5.1 is a self-assessment to help you determine your skill level in dealing with difficult or disruptive students. For each skill in the first columns, rate yourself on a scale of one to ten—one being very limited and ten being very prepared. Be critical of your skills in each area and rate each skill honestly. Once you've finished the assessment, look at the skills with the lowest scores. Note some strategies or resources from the following list that you could use to gain knowledge in these areas. Some examples of resources might include:

▶ Working with your principal or grade- or course-level team

▶ Talking with a behavioral interventionist

▶ Working with a special education teacher, your mentor, or a coach

▶ Reading books and articles related to the skill area

▶ Attending professional development related to the skill area

| Skill for Dealing With Difficult or Disruptive Students | Your Level of Skill in This Area (1 = Very Limited, 5 = Somewhat Prepared, 10 = Very Prepared) | Resources for Addressing Skill Limitation |
|---|---|---|
| A clear understanding of the behaviors required to be successful in your classroom | 1  2  3  4  5  6  7  8  9  10 | |
| The ability to emotionally disconnect from the problem behavior or issue | 1  2  3  4  5  6  7  8  9  10 | |
| The ability to observe and accurately describe the problem behavior | 1  2  3  4  5  6  7  8  9  10 | |
| An understanding of the bigger picture and the patience to resolve the problem behavior in a step-by-step manner | 1  2  3  4  5  6  7  8  9  10 | |
| The ability to design and implement an improvement plan to reduce the disruptive or difficult behavior | 1  2  3  4  5  6  7  8  9  10 | |
| The ability to break the desired behavior into small, teachable parts | 1  2  3  4  5  6  7  8  9  10 | |
| The ability to examine all issues impacting a problem behavior— including your own teaching | 1  2  3  4  5  6  7  8  9  10 | |

Figure 5.1: Essential skills to deal with difficult or disruptive students.

*Visit **go.solution-tree.com/instruction** to download a free reproducible version of this figure.*

## Identifying the Issues

Once you better understand your personal strengths and limitations related to managing difficult and disruptive situations, you can take the next step—to examine what is happening in difficult situations with students. It's crucial that you find a way to focus on the exact behavior that's causing the problem. You can do this through focused observations in your own classroom or by asking an outside person, such as a coach or mentor, to observe the situation in your classroom.

When you encounter a behavior situation or problem in your classroom, try to first understand the cause or motivation behind the behavior. Also keep in mind that something outside of the school could be causing the problem. You may want to communicate with others who are in contact with the student—parents, family members, and so on—to see what sorts of issues they are encountering with a student and how they deal with them. Using similar strategies or working together to address the same behavior might help minimize the misbehavior. Teachers have sometimes developed behavior-management plans in conjunction with parents so everyone is on the same page and working together to improve the situation.

Always look at the possibility of structural or learning environment difficulties when tackling a problem. Is the classroom well organized? Are you clear in delivering directions? Are you consistent in handling situations? Does the nature of the content area contribute to the problem? What have the students encountered before coming to your class that could be contributing to their issues? These and other questions will help you see if you can effectively manage the problem behavior.

If you have the ability to objectively step back from the situation, you may be able to see some of the trends or patterns that could be contributing to a student's behavior problems. Use the form in figure 5.2 to conduct an objective observation of your classroom or a colleague's classroom to look for issues that may be contributing to student behavior problems.

Sometimes, student behaviors don't lend themselves to time studies because some behaviors don't occur on a schedule or may not happen regularly. Other behaviors may happen so frequently that keeping track of every occurrence would soon fill the whole page. In these cases, you may benefit from a more general, narrative observation. Figure 5.3 shows a form for an observation where time is not recorded.

| Behavior | Time Exhibited | Time Exhibited | Time Exhibited | Time Exhibited | Time Exhibited | Time Exhibited | Time Exhibited |
|---|---|---|---|---|---|---|---|
| | | | | | | | |
| | | | | | | | |
| | | | | | | | |
| | | | | | | | |
| | | | | | | | |

**Student name:** _____ **Teacher:** _____

**Class period:** _____ **Suspected or potential behavior issue:** _____

1. Describe the specific behaviors you observed the student exhibiting.

2. Does any other behavior or issue seem to trigger the behavior?

3. What were the other students' reactions to this behavior? How did you/the teacher react to the behavior?

4. What patterns did you observe in either the student's behavior or your/the teacher's reaction to the behavior?

Figure 5.2: Difficult behavior observation form.

*Visit **go.solution-tree.com/instruction** to download a free reproducible version of this figure.*

**Student name:** _____ **Teacher:** _____

**Class period:** _____ **Suspected or potential behavior issue:** _____

1. In general, what behaviors did the student exhibit?

2. Was there an order or sequence in the exhibited behaviors?

3. What seemed to promote or trigger these behaviors?

4. What was your reaction and the other students' reaction and the reaction of the other students when these behaviors were exhibited?

5. Did any other patterns or clues to the reason for the behaviors appear during the observation?

6. Did you notice anything else while observing that may be helpful to you or the teacher in dealing with these behaviors?

Figure 5.3: Narrative behavior observation form.

*Visit **go.solution-tree.com/instruction** to download a free reproducible version of this figure.*

## Using Classroom-Management Problem Solvers

In many cases, student disruptions are the result of small, connected problems that have been left unchecked. In our work with schools, we have developed a classroom-management problem solver. This resource describes common problematic behaviors along with a series of strategies and directions the teacher can use to resolve them. The problem solver is designed to be a practical, quick reference for busy teachers, so it purposely does not contain a lot of background or theory. What we present here is a condensed and straightforward tool.

The ideas and strategies in the problem solver are an example of the many ways teachers can modify student behavior using some basic techniques. Choosing which strategies to implement depends on the student, the issue, your classroom dynamics, and other considerations. Use your best judgment in selecting and implementing the strategies. What works well for one professional in one setting may not work in your situation, and a strategy that helped manage and modify one student's behavior in the past may not fit another student with the same behavior's needs. Keep the following in mind as you use this resource.

> ▸ **Review the ideas and strategies carefully:** Make sure you understand how to implement a strategy before moving forward. Since the resource is meant to be a starting point, be sure to become familiar with best practices in strategy areas or work with your colleagues or your building principal as you implement strategies.

> ▸ **Select one or two strategies to focus on first:** Give yourself the time and freedom to see how they unfold before moving on to other ideas. If you select one or two strategies to implement in response to a behavior problem, you should stick with them for a couple of weeks before deciding they don't work. Making changes takes time and dedication. Remember, in addition to you learning the new technique, the students will also need a chance to get acclimated to the new idea.

> ▸ **Be ready for the implementation dip that always occurs when a new idea is implemented in a school or classroom:** Many people find that the new strategy works well for a while (because it is new) but then fades out after a short period of time. Set yourself up on a plan and review your progress regarding the new idea. Reteach or review the plan periodically.

> ▸ **Gather data regarding student progress:** Use these data to gauge the success of your implementation.

As you move forward, keep your principal informed about your implementation. He or she can be very helpful as you continue to help your students be successful in your classroom.

The problem-solver resource is divided into seven separate tables (tables 5.1 to 5.7, pages 103–106) that cover the following topics.

1. Students who are not maintaining attention in the classroom (table 5.1)

2. Students who are not following classroom procedures (table 5.2, page 104)

3. Students who are not following directions in the classroom (table 5.3, page 104)

4. Students who are not prepared for learning (table 5.4, page 105)

5. Students having difficulty with assignment completion (table 5.5, page 105)

6. Students who are oppositional to teacher authority (table 5.6, page 106)

7. Students who are over-reactive and need to be calmed (table 5.7, page 106)

The tables are designed to be used either individually or along with your teams and colleagues. In each table, there is a blank area for you to add other ideas and strategies that you find beneficial or to keep notes about what works with individual students. It is important in the area of student discipline and classroom management to share ideas that are effective among all the professionals who work with individual students to maintain a consistent response to problematic behavior. Sharing helps you and your team better meet student needs and set a collaborative tone for the entire building.

### Table 5.1: Maintaining Attention in the Classroom

| Problem | Proactive Ideas to Prevent or Positively Impact the Problem |
|---|---|
| Students are hard to get focused at the beginning of class. | • Provide a transition activity for students when they enter the room to get them focused right away.<br>• Stand at the door to welcome students and remind them to sit down and get started with their work.<br>• Provide soft music as the students enter the room. Turn the music down at the start of class as a signal to get started.<br>• Provide an audible signal to get students' attention at the beginning of the class period.<br>• Teach a procedure for entering the classroom quietly and starting work right away. |
| Building and colleague ideas and strategies: | |

*Visit **go.solution-tree.com/instruction** to download a free reproducible version of this table.*

## Table 5.2: Ensuring Students Follow Classroom Procedures

| Problem | Proactive Ideas to Prevent or Positively Impact the Problem |
|---|---|
| Students have difficulty following prescribed procedures. | • Think through all required processes, and design them to be straightforward and direct.<br>• Post the required procedures for various activities in the front of the room.<br>• Provide picture guides to illustrate required procedures that students can look at.<br>• Post picture or verbal procedural guides by stations or centers.<br>• Assign a student to explain and follow up on procedures and directions with peers at a center or station.<br>• Eliminate unnecessary or extra steps in procedures or processes to ensure student success.<br>• Before sending students to activities, have them review procedures in small groups or pairs. |
| Building and colleague ideas and strategies: | |

*Visit **go.solution-tree.com/instruction** to download a free reproducible version of this table.*

## Table 5.3: Following Directions in the Classroom

| Problem | Proactive Ideas to Prevent or Positively Impact the Problem |
|---|---|
| Students have difficulty following directions from the teacher. | • Review directions to ensure clarity.<br>• Provide only three directions at a time to students.<br>• After providing directions, have students review or restate them in small groups.<br>• When giving directions, provide nonverbal gestures and signals to assist in understanding the directions.<br>• Use written reminders of directions at stations or centers.<br>• Look at students when giving directions. Stop and wait for all students to focus on you before starting directions.<br>• Approach or stand by students who traditionally have trouble following directions. Once they get back on task, step away. Use this strategy sparingly.<br>• Ask selected students to repeat parts or all of the directions.<br>• Ask selected students to demonstrate implementation of the directions before others start to implement them.<br>• If noise starts or students look away while you are giving directions, stop and refocus them.<br>• Praise or reinforce students immediately who followed directions correctly after you have given them. |
| Building and colleague ideas and strategies: | |

*Visit **go.solution-tree.com/instruction** to download a free reproducible version of this table.*

## Table 5.4: Being Prepared for Learning

| Problem | Proactive Ideas to Prevent or Positively Impact the Problem |
|---|---|
| Students come to class but don't have the materials or supplies needed for learning activities. | • Provide a materials reminder at the door or classroom or learning station.<br>• Post a required material list on student desks or tables.<br>• Review needed materials at the beginning of the class or period.<br>• Provide a buddy system to assist students in having required materials in place.<br>• Provide a place where extra materials can be "purchased" by students with currency you issue as a reward for positive behavior.<br>• Develop material storage locations, such as bins and folders, where students can keep materials in class or work stations.<br>• Have all needed learning materials for everyone stored in a community bin that all students pull from when needed. At the end of class, all materials are returned to the bin. |
| Building and colleague ideas and strategies: | |

*Visit **go.solution-tree.com/instruction** to download a free reproducible version of this table.*

## Table 5.5: Completing Assignments

| Problem | Proactive Ideas to Prevent or Positively Impact the Problem |
|---|---|
| Students have difficulty completing or turning in assignments. | • Provide structured work time in class. For example, set the expectation that a certain number of problems need to be completed before dismissal.<br>• Find out why the homework is not being completed. Ask sincerely and let students know that you care.<br>• Allow students to work in teams or pairs on homework in class if they reach a certain level of completion.<br>• Provide an assistance center that students can attend if they need help.<br>• Require students who have a history of poor work completion to check in with you at the end of the day regarding homework completion.<br>• Allow students to make copies of materials in order to write on them or highlight them.<br>• Require students to attend homework help sessions.<br>• Call the students' homes in the evenings who traditionally have difficulty completing homework to check on their progress.<br>• For complex or difficult assignments, require parts due at different times or stages.<br>• Provide a weekly assignment overview on the board or post assignments on your website to allow students to plan ahead.<br>• Use significant adults (coaches, academic sponsors, club sponsors, and so on) to help encourage students to complete work. |
| Building and colleague ideas and strategies: | |

*Visit **go.solution-tree.com/instruction** to download a free reproducible version of this table.*

Table 5.6: Complying With Teacher Authority

| Problem | Proactive Ideas to Prevent or Positively Impact the Problem |
|---|---|
| Students show a lack of regard for teacher authority, do not have respect for the teacher, or are defiant with teacher directives. | • Think through classroom requirements and provide students with choices whenever possible.<br>• Resist arguments and handle potential problems discreetly in the classroom.<br>• Watch for indications that students may become confrontational, and don't allow them to take you down the confrontational path.<br>• Use reflecting or paraphrasing to let students know you understand their feelings or emotions and to help redirect their energy.<br>• If there is a severe or explosive confrontation, get the assistance of colleagues.<br>• If there is a severe or explosive confrontation, remove other students from the classroom before dealing with disruptive students.<br>• Use appropriate humor to de-escalate behavior. Be careful not to use sarcasm with students.<br>• Deal with defiance outside of class or out of the view of other students.<br>• Model respectful behavior to the student.<br>• Dress and act professionally in and out of the classroom.<br>• Work with your coach or mentor to develop ideas.<br>• Set up a meeting with the dean of students or the assistant principal and the students to develop a plan.<br>• Set up a meeting with the parents or guardians and the student to develop a plan. |
| Building and colleague ideas and strategies: | |

*Visit **go.solution-tree.com/instruction** to download a free reproducible version of this table.*

Table 5.7: Keeping Over-Reactive Students Calm

| Problem | Proactive Ideas to Prevent or Positively Impact the Problem |
|---|---|
| Students become anxious or exhibit impulsive behaviors in class. | • Work with students in advance of the problem to understand what sets them off.<br>• Develop a private signal to let the students know they are beginning to over-react.<br>• Break the day or instructional period into parts to help maintain calmness.<br>• Use a timer to help students self-monitor on-task behavior.<br>• Provide a small marker board or notepad for students to write questions or comments rather than blurt them out in class. Then provide regular times to review these notes with the student.<br>• Teach students appropriate on-task behaviors.<br>• Provide a peer to help students maintain focus.<br>• Provide calming music for the class to help keep emotions in check.<br>• Teach class relaxation and breathing exercises, and implement them regularly during the day or period.<br>• Provide students with a time-out area or a place to go when they feel out of control. |
| Building and colleague ideas and strategies: | |

*Visit **go.solution-tree.com/instruction** to download a free reproducible version of this table.*

As you try the various strategies outlined in the problem-solver charts, keep in mind that not every strategy will work in every situation. You may need to work with your principal, a special education teacher, a behavioral specialist or interventionist, a school psychologist, your coach, your mentor, or some other knowledgeable professional to generate the exact strategies you need to address the behavior issues you encounter in specific students. Some behaviors can be very difficult (or nearly impossible) to address. Be sure to involve the parents in helping to solve the issue and in any discussions for additional strategies or services. If this is the case and you find that you cannot address an issue, work with others to get the student specialized help.

## Reinforcing Positive Changes

In chapter 4, we talked about the use of reinforcement theory to help students learn behavioral expectations in the classroom. We learned about three types of reinforcement—positive, negative, and extinction. Reinforcement theory—specifically positive reinforcement—can be very helpful in managing severely disruptive behaviors. It can be effective because the student is getting something he or she desires for exhibiting appropriate behaviors. An important part of modifying a behavior is providing lots of positive reinforcement for a student in the early stages of learning a new behavior.

In this section, we focus on how to identify and use positive reinforcement to help reshape difficult or disruptive student behavior. Following is a list of strategies to identify possible positive reinforcers for students.

▸ Think about what you know about a student. What might he or she desire as a reinforcer? Some students may desire attention, recognition, or more interaction with adults. Examples might include lunch with the teacher, public praise for appropriate behavior, and personal notes from the teacher. Some students desire positive attention from their peer group. In these cases, reinforcers that allow students to earn some sort of privilege for their peers or a small group of friends work well.

▸ Consult with people inside the school who have contact with the student; ask for their ideas on what might motivate the student. Some students might have a particular interest in certain topics, such as a specific animal. Being able to read or watch a movie about a favorite thing, hobby, sports team, and so on as a reward can be a reinforcer.

▸ Observe the student in settings outside of the classroom. Look for situations where the student seems particularly interested or motivated. Use this knowledge to develop a preliminary list of reinforcers. Let's say you notice a student is particularly interested in football. You might incorporate some football-related reinforcers, such as earning football cards, being able to watch a portion of a recorded football game, getting to meet a local high school football star, or something else easy to manage that's related to football.

▶ Contact the student's parents or guardians to find out what motivates their child. Talk with your mentor, your coach, or a colleague who has worked with the student in the past to identify possible topics that would be motivational for the student.

▶ If you administered an interest inventory to your students, use this information to see what hobbies and interests the student has identified. This will help determine possible reinforcers.

▶ Think about conversations, interactions, reading, and other things you have seen the student do with others at the school. Use this information to generate a list.

▶ Meet with the student and find out what might be interesting or motivating for him or her. We have found this to be most effective when we frame the conversation in the context of statements like:

- If you could do anything in school, what would you choose?
- If we gave you a chance to earn something for changing your behavior, what would you choose?
- What do you think might motivate you to change and improve your behavior?

Figure 5.4 is a worksheet to use when identifying positive reinforcers.

---

**Student name:** _____ **Grade level:** _____

**Teachers:** _____

_____

**Specific behavior to be modified:** _____

1. What areas of interest have you seen this student express or exhibit inside or outside of the classroom?

2. In relation to these interests, what types of specific activities or strategies might be the most motivating to be used in changing the behavior of this student?

3. Of the list you generated, which would make the most sense to be used within the school in a behavior plan to help modify the behavior of this student?

4. List the possible reinforcers you generated in a hierarchy from simplest and least costly to implement to the most complex and most costly to provide to the student.

---

Figure 5.4: Worksheet for identifying positive reinforcers.

*Visit **go.solution-tree.com/instruction** to download a free reproducible version of this figure.*

Once you have identified the positive reinforcers, implement them the next time the student shows positive progress. Figure 5.5 provides a template to help you track your implementation of positive reinforcers and their impact.

**Directions:** An important part of modifying a behavior is providing lots of positive reinforcement for a student in the early stages of learning a new behavior. Use this form to track your delivery of positive reinforcers for the student as she or he changes the behavior.

**Student name:** _____

**Specific targeted behavior:** _____

**Selected reinforcement:** _____

In the following table, write the number of times you reinforced the desired behavior each school day. Record the week's total in the last row.

| Day | Times Reinforced |
| --- | --- |
| Monday | |
| Tuesday | |
| Wednesday | |
| Thursday | |
| Friday | |
| Week total | |

Figure 5.5: Template for tracking positive reinforcement.

*Visit **go.solution-tree.com/instruction** to download a free reproducible version of this figure.*

Once you complete the template, reflect on how often you're positively reinforcing a desired behavior. If you are providing meaningful and regular positive reinforcement and the student is still exhibiting the behavior, you may need to change either the positive reinforcement or the schedule that you're using to deliver it.

## Using Behavior Contracts

Another effective way to manage a disruptive or difficult student is to develop a behavior contract. A behavior contract is a personalized plan that you can develop with a student, the student and his or her parents, the student and other teachers, or any combination of these.

In developing a behavior contract, you should target the most disruptive behaviors. In targeting these behaviors, you should first be sure to specifically describe them and the problems they are causing in your classroom. Once you identify the specific behaviors, put together a list of possible reinforcers and possible consequences. Identify both reinforcers and consequences to help the student to reduce and then eventually stop the disruptive or difficult behavior.

Remember, consequences should be instructional in nature. They should fit the student's infraction. They should be simple and straightforward to implement and maintain the dignity of the student. And, most important, you should be sure to follow through and implement the consequences you have determined. Figure 5.6 is a template for developing a behavior contract. The best contracts are developed with the student's involvement. After all, if the contract is an agreement that the student will abide by, he or she should have some say in the final product. If a student doesn't have the skills to participate in the development of the contract, you and other adults in the school can develop an initial draft and present it to the student.

I, _____ (student's name), have been disruptive in school. My disruptive behavior includes the following.

- _____
- _____
- _____

These inappropriate behaviors have to stop. In stopping these behaviors, I will do the following.

- _____
- _____
- _____

If I fail to stop my inappropriate behaviors, the following will occur.

- First time: _____
- Second time: _____
- Third time: _____
- Fourth time: _____
- Fifth time: _____

Include details about the conditions of the contract, specific positive reinforcers, and so on. This list could also include any specific rewards the student might be able to earn by changing the disruptive behavior.

We agree to follow this contract.

Student: _____

Teacher: _____

Principal: _____

Parent: _____

Figure 5.6: Behavior contract planning template.

*Visit **go.solution-tree.com/instruction** to download a free reproducible version of this figure.*

Figures 5.7 and 5.8 (page 112) show examples of completed behavior contracts for an elementary student and a secondary student, respectively.

---

I, _David Morris_ , have been disruptive in school. My disruptive behavior includes the following:

- *I have been talking and making comments when I am not supposed to or do not have my teacher's permission to talk or make comments.*
- *I have been making inappropriate or off-task comments.*

These inappropriate behaviors have to stop. In stopping these behaviors, I will do the following:

- *Raise my hand and wait for the teacher or supervisor to call on me before making a comment.*
- *When making a comment or asking a question, I will only share things that are productive or based on the lesson or assignment.*
- *I will not make comments that are funny or entertaining to others during the time the teacher is presenting lessons or the class is working.*

If I fail to stop my inappropriate behaviors, the following will occur:

- First time—*Receive a verbal warning*
- Second time—*Lose fifteen minutes of recess and visit with teacher during that time*
- Third time—*Lose the whole recess and visit with teacher during that time*
- Fourth time—*Go to Principal Meyers's office and get a call home to my parents*
- Fifth time—*Go to Saturday detention*

If I am able to change my behavior, I can earn one point for each half day I meet expectations. The points can be spent for the following:

- Ten points—*A prize from the principal's basket and a call home to let parents know*
- Twenty-five points—*Ten minutes of extra recess for the entire class and a call home to let parents know*
- Fifty points—*Lunch with the principal and a friend and a call home to let parents know*
- One hundred points—*A special reward from the principal*

This consequence list will start new each day. When I am able to control my inappropriate behavior, I will be able to earn positive points. For each half day that I behave appropriately according to the conditions in this contract, I will receive a point. Once I accumulate points, I can use them for items and privileges based on a plan I develop between my teachers and myself.

We agree to follow this contract.

Student : _David Morris_

Teacher: _Keisha Abbiati_

Principal: _Tyrion Meyers_

Parent: _Cindy Morris_

---

Figure 5.7: Sample elementary behavior contract.

I, _Yara Pike_, have been disruptive in school. My disruptive behavior includes the following:

- *I have been distracting other students from their learning when I come back to the classroom from an outside activity.*
- *I have been arguing with my teachers when they call me on my off-task behavior.*

These inappropriate behaviors have to stop. In stopping these behaviors, I will do the following:

- *Enter the room quietly without disturbing others.*
- *When entering the room, go right to my work station, making minimal eye contact with other students. I will also try not to distract them from their learning by getting my materials out quickly and getting right to work.*
- *I'll respond positively to and acknowledge my teacher's feedback on my performance in entering the room.*

If I fail to stop my inappropriate behaviors, the following will occur:

- First time—*Receive a verbal reminder*
- Second time—*Meet privately with my teacher for fifteen minutes to discuss the problem and practice the appropriate behavior*
- Third time—*Call home, inform my parents of the situation, and my plan to address it*
- Fourth time—*Talk with principal and teacher to develop other consequences and strategies to address my problem*
- Fifth time—*Be removed from from classroom for a minimum of three days, call home, and develop a re-entry plan to address behavior issues before returning to the classroom*

If I am able to change my behavior, I can earn rewards. These rewards can include:

- *Free time after five days of good behavior*
- *A free period in the technology lab helping other students after ten days of good behavior*
- *Three hours in the video production lab helping to develop the weekly information video*

This consequence list will start new each week. When I am able to control my inappropriate behavior, I will be able to earn positive points. For each half day that I behave appropriately according to the conditions in this contract, I will receive a point. Once I accumulate points, I can use them for items and privileges based on a plan I develop between my teachers and myself.

We agree to follow this contract.

Student: _Yara Pike_

Teacher: *Lynne Boyle*

Principal: Mohammed Z. B. Halim

Parent: *Andrew Pike*

Figure 5.8: Sample secondary behavior contract.

# Working Productively With Parents on Behavioral Issues

Parents (and guardians) can be a great ally to teachers who are dealing with students who are exhibiting disruptive or difficult behaviors. In many cases, when you talk with the parent, you'll find that he or she is dealing with similar issues at home and may be struggling with how to get the student under control. As you begin to think about how you might engage the parents in the conversation, there are some special considerations you will want to take into account.

## Communicating With Parents

When working with parents or guardians, it is essential to develop good rapport and a strong working relationship. Consider the following strategies to develop a good working relationship with the parents of your students.

- **Consider holding information-gathering conferences with parents early in the year, rather than just presenting problems during a traditional conference:** Many schools are restructuring their conference schedule to allow teachers to hold early conferences to gather information from parents related to their perceptions of their child's strengths, needs, and educational experiences. If these conferences are conducted as information-gathering sessions for the teacher, effective parental relationships can develop as a result.

- **Call parents for good news and positive information about their child:** You are probably not the first person to experience issues with this student. The parents might have had several years of negative communication from schools. Consider calling the parents of potentially disruptive students *before* they start getting into a lot of trouble. Several calls placed in advance of difficulties can go a long way in building a positive relationship before issues become problematic.

- **Frame issues in the best interest of the student when talking to a parent:** Parents are always looking to help their child be successful. When you frame the issue based on what's best for their child, they will know that you are an advocate and acting in the best interest of their son or daughter.

- **When parents bring you concerns, use framing as a strategy to focus the conversation on the major issues:** Framing can be an effective tool to use in helping keep any conversation on track but is especially helpful in letting a parent know that you are interested in successfully resolving issues plus building a collaborative relationship. Framing statements like, "Let's talk about the major issues your son reported and how we can work together to resolve them" or "I know there have been many problems in the past. Let's focus on the three that we can work out together right away and make a plan to address the others at a future date" help parents understand the scope of the conversation plus help keep the process on track. As you work to resolve the most immediate issues, you also help set a problem-solving tone that may have been absent in previous years or settings.

▸ **Fully listen to what the parent has to say before interrupting or refuting his or her perspective:** In many cases, students' parents or guardians have not been listened to fully in past conversations. This causes frustration and defensiveness. If you listen fully, then bring forth other perspectives or ideas, you communicate to the parent that you are interested in hearing what she or he has to say while maintaining your own perspective. This type of action shows the parent that you care and will consider alternatives.

## Informing Parents When a Behavior Problem Occurs

In many cases, the telephone is the most efficient and effective mode of communicating information to parents and guardians. Phone communications can be highly effective or negative and not very productive. Keep the following considerations in mind as you contact parents via phone in relation to student behavior issues.

▸ **Use the phone strategically:** Don't just pick up the phone every time there's an issue. You may want to wait until the end of the day or communicate with the parent when he or she picks up the student after school. It may be hard for some parents to take a call at work, so you may want to plan your call accordingly.

▸ **Whenever possible, involve the student in communicating the initial behavior information to parents:** This is effective because it's good for the parent to hear the issue directly from his or her child, and if there is any negative reaction, the child will be the first one to hear it. In implementing this strategy, you may need to rehearse the phone call with the student before actually contacting the parent. After the student has communicated the initial information, let him or her know that you need to talk to the parent and convey the rest of the information required for the situation.

▸ **Use framing when calling parents:** Let them know the intent of the call and what you hope to accomplish as a result of this immediate communication.

▸ **If possible, share how you have dealt with the situation or your plan to address the issue at school:** By sharing the results versus asking parents to solve the issue, you convey your credibility. If you have not yet been able to solve the issue, use the phone call to inform the parent and set up a face-to-face meeting where you can work together to develop a plan to address the student's behavior.

▸ **Avoid apologizing for the phone contact or blaming parents for their child's behavior:** These practices set up a defensive feeling that can set a negative tone and diminish the relationship between you and the parent. Nobody likes to get a call blaming him or her for a situation that happens outside the parent's control (at school). Be cordial and at all times stay professional to build a partnership with the parent.

▸ **Keep the phone call clear and concise:** Write down the major points you want to address before you call so you can stay focused and on point. Parents are busy too and want you to get to the point while conveying the major information they need to know. When nearing the end of the call, be sure that the parent understands what happened and what will happen as a result. You may want to set up a plan to follow up in a couple of days to assess how things are going or meet to develop a more comprehensive plan to work together to help address the student's behavior issues.

▸ **At the end of the call, thank the parents for their time and remind them of the longer-term goal:** For example, stating, "Thank you for your time. I know together we will be able to help Michele get her behavior under control" communicates that you are grateful for their assistance and that you think they will help make a difference in the student's behavior.

Let's see how an elementary teacher, Jaquana, handles a conversation with the parents of a disruptive student.

> *Jaquana has encountered an issue with one of her students, Courtney. She decides that because of the situation, it's best to call Courtney's father, Bill, immediately after she addresses the issue with Courtney. Jaquana lets Courtney know that she is going to also be talking to her dad. Jaquana can see that this makes*

*Courtney nervous, so she helps Courtney develop an outline and rehearse what Courtney will say to her dad.*

*Jaquana makes the call.*

*Jaquana: Hello, Mr. Smith. This is Ms. Arella, Courtney's teacher. How are you today?*

*Bill: I'm fine. What's up?*

*Jaquana: Courtney had an issue in class today. I thought we should call you. We want to let you know what happened and what Courtney and I have determined we will do to address the issue.*

*Bill: Okay.*

*Courtney: Hi, Dad. Today, during our work time, I got mad at Jeremy. I took his assignment paper away from him and ripped it up.*

*Bill: Okay. Why did you do that?*

*Courtney: I don't know. I guess I just lost it. Ms. Arella and I came up with a plan for what I did. I will be writing Jeremy an apology note. Since he had to take time to redo the assignment, I'll help him to make up that time. Plus, Ms. Arella and I wrote a plan so this won't happen again. I'll bring it home tonight.*

*Bill: Thanks for telling me about this. I'm disappointed that this happened. You know this is not how we solve things in our family. We'll talk about this more when I get home tonight.*

*Courtney: I know. I'm sorry I had to bother you. Ms. Arella wants to talk to you now.*

*Jaquana: I think Courtney and I have addressed the situation, but I just wanted you to know about it. She said she just got upset, but I'm happy that we were able to put together a plan so it hopefully won't happen again. Thank you for taking the time to listen and work with Courtney. I'll be sure to keep you informed if any other issues arise. Have a good rest of the day.*

In this example, you can see how Jaquana handled the communication and involved Courtney in the conversation. Since Jaquana and Courtney wrote outlines and rehearsed what they were going to say, the conversation stayed focused and productive.

## Developing a Plan for School-Home Efforts

Parents and guardians can be pivotal in helping bring student behaviors under control if they are used effectively as a resource. In most cases, they have information and experiences that can be useful in following through in behavior-management plans. Before deciding what kinds of follow-up strategies you may ask parents to do at home, consider the following factors:

▸ Length of time parent has been dealing with the issue at home

▸ Parent's behavior-management skills

▸ Amount of time the parent has available to work with his or her child

▸ Amount of collaboration and support the parent has with the teacher and school

▸ Severity and intensity of the behavior issue

▸ Number of behavior issues

▸ Past experiences the parent has had in dealing with the behavior issue, including strategies they have tried to address the behavior

▸ Philosophical match between the parent and the school in dealing with the behavior. Does the parent agree that the behavior is a problem? Implement your own plan for addressing the behavior, but don't be offended if the parent doesn't agree with you or support you.

▸ Ability of the parent to stay focused on the issue. Some parents may have some of the same behaviors you are trying to moderate in their child. Other parents may have their own issues to deal with and may not have the psychological strength to stay focused on a plan. Other parents may be so busy working several jobs or managing their other children that they can't take on any more issues. Don't take their lack of interest or support personally. Plan how you can move forward on your own if necessary.

Keep in mind that managing a student's behavior can sometimes be easier for school professionals than for parents. You may need to actually teach parents how to follow through at home and address the issues with their children.

Following are some specific strategies for addressing behavior at home to support the behavior management going on at school.

▸ Assist the parent in developing a plan to follow up on the issues you are addressing at school: If you can find a way for both you and the parent to focus on the same behaviors, it can be very effective. While you can't solve what is happening at home, the united focus will send a message to the student that you are working together.

▸ Ask the parent to provide feedback on the student's behavior-management form, card, or contract on a regular basis: Normally, this involvement requires that the parent talk with his or her child about the day (or behavior period) and how things are going. Talk with the parent about his or her interactions with the student to ensure that both of you are using the same approach to resolve the issue.

▸ Encourage parents to keep a communication journal: In this journal, the parent will keep track of conversations he or she has had with the child in relation to the behaviors outlined in the behavior-management plan. The parent can look for patterns in the communications and bring the journal to meetings with the teacher and other school staff to discuss the progress and the issues related to the student behaviors.

▸ Arrange for regular communication about the student's progress on the plan: You should communicate regularly to ensure the plan is working. This can be done on the phone, in person, or through email.

When developing your plan to work with parents, you need to be clear and specific about the behaviors you want to change, use regular communication, schedule follow ups, and determine your indicators of success. Working together with the parent should be rewarding and enlightening and keep progress moving in a positive direction.

## Summary and Reflection

In this chapter, we presented tools and strategies to identify and begin to diminish difficult and disruptive student behaviors by addressing the behavior with contracts and behavior-management plans.

As you reflect on the contents of this chapter, take a few minutes to respond to the following questions.

▸ What are some common behavior issues in the classroom? What strategies can you use to help students avoid those issues that are most common in your classrooms?

▸ What are some of the items to include in a behavior contract? How can a behavior contract help get disruptive and difficult student behavior under control?

▸ Why is it so important to identify the specific behavior issues of a student before developing an intervention to deal with these behaviors?

▸ What are some strategies to get parents involved in a positive and proactive manner when dealing with the behavior issues of their child?

In the next chapter, we will focus on curriculum management and how thriving new teachers design their instruction around learning standards and targets.

# chapter 6

# Tackling Curriculum Management

*Marvin, a new middle school teacher, is getting ready to teach a unit on measurement. In order to prepare for the unit, Marvin checks the district-curriculum guide for the standards and learning objectives that students are supposed to achieve in this area. He can see that his part of the curriculum moves the students into a more complex application of measurement.*

*In preparing for the start of the unit, Marvin works with his colleagues to see if they have developed a preassessment he can use to see what skills and content knowledge his students have before he starts the unit. This will help him know what areas may need more focus or emphasis.*

*In developing his plan for the unit, Marvin includes a list of learning targets that the students need to master. He knows that it is important for them to understand what they will be learning and how they will be reaching the targets.*

In this scenario, Marvin develops his unit, determining what he will teach, based on the outcome the students need to reach. This focus on state or districtwide standards and learning objectives ensures that all students are meeting the same goals and learning what has been deemed most critical for their subject or grade level. By helping students understand what they need to know through learning targets, Marvin reinforces the expected learning and helps his students to be invested and successful in mastering it.

Curriculum management is an important skill for becoming a thriving new teacher. It can be difficult at first to design your teaching around curricular standards and learning objectives. To do so, you will need to understand the concept of standards and how standards guide your teaching, what learning objectives and targets are, and the importance of planning lessons and units around these elements as well as the elements involved in a good unit and lesson plan.

## Defining Standards and Their Importance

*Standards* are specific, clear descriptions of what students should know or be able to do at various grade levels and within various content areas. They focus on what learning students are to acquire or processes students will be able to complete during various stages of their education. Standards typically do not focus on specific teaching methods or assessment strategies. See figure 6.1 for a small example of a section of the Common Core English language arts standards for grade 6 literacy.

---

**CCSS.ELA-Literacy.W.6.2**
Write informative/explanatory texts to examine a topic and convey ideas, concepts, and information through the selection, organization, and analysis of relevant content.

**CCSS.ELA-Literacy.W.6.2a**
Introduce a topic; organize ideas, concepts, and information, using strategies such as definition, classification, comparison/contrast, and cause/effect; include formatting (e.g., headings), graphics (e.g., charts, tables), and multimedia when useful to aiding comprehension.

**CCSS.ELA-Literacy.W.6.2b**
Develop the topic with relevant facts, definitions, concrete details, quotations, or other information and examples.

**CCSS.ELA-Literacy.W.6.2c**
Use appropriate transitions to clarify the relationships among ideas and concepts.

**CCSS.ELA-Literacy.W.6.2d**
Use precise language and domain-specific vocabulary to inform about or explain the topic.

**CCSS.ELA-Literacy.W.6.2e**
Establish and maintain a formal style.

**CCSS.ELA-Literacy.W.6.2f**
Provide a concluding statement or section that follows from the information or explanation presented.

---

*Source: National Governors Association Center for Best Practices & Council of Chief State School Officers, 2010.*

Figure 6.1: Sample Common Core English language arts standards.

Standards can be defined by a school or district or at the state or national level. At the time this book was written, forty-two U.S. states, the District of Columbia, four U.S. territories, and the U.S. Department of Defense Education Activity have adopted the Common Core State Standards (Common Core State Standards Initiative, 2015). Clearly defined standards allow you to understand the expectations for your teaching during an academic year. Most teachers using the CCSS allow the standards to guide their planning for units, lessons, and assessments. Students are also assessed every year based on the standards they should achieve.

## Defining Objectives and Learning Targets

*Objectives* are specific descriptions of the short-term goal or goals of a particular lesson. Objectives typically focus on the lesson level and the teaching that will occur within a particular lesson. Objectives do specify the content, the teaching methods, and the assessment that teachers will use during instruction. Objectives typically focus on the teacher and what the teacher will do to assist students in the learning. Objectives help guide the teacher and help the teacher to determine if the students have met the learning requirements of a particular lesson.

Figure 6.2 shows several objectives related to the English language arts standards featured in figure 6.1.

---

**CCSS.ELA-Literacy.W.6.2**
Write informative/explanatory texts to examine a topic and convey ideas, concepts, and information through the selection, organization, and analysis of relevant content.

**Lesson Objectives**
These objectives could be for three separate lessons or implemented in the same lesson.

1. After a lesson on the components of writing an effective informational paper, students will be able to utilize a scoring guide to identify the major components in sample informational papers provided by the teacher with 100 percent accuracy.

2. After a lesson on writing informational papers, the students will select a topic and write the introductory paragraph to an informational paper with 100 percent proficiency in utilizing the components of topic selection criteria, clear topic description, and clear topic analysis based on a scoring rubric shared in class.

3. Following a review of the essential elements of effective informational papers, students will be able to review and edit an informational introductory paragraph they developed earlier using a scoring rubric shared in a previous class.

*Source for standard: NGA & CCSSO, 2010.*

---

Figure 6.2: Sample lesson objectives for a Common Core English language arts standard.

The three objectives provided in figure 6.2 illustrate the teacher level of focus on learning. These objectives break the standard into smaller, more teachable processes. They are very specific and give the teacher the exact content to present to reach the standard. The objectives also provide the specific measurement or assessment that students are to use to show the teacher that they have learned or mastered the objectives. The objectives work together to help the students attain the larger standard.

*Learning targets* describe what students will learn within a lesson and how they will demonstrate that learning. The key to the success of a learning target is that it is presented specifically for students and is written in student-friendly language. Learning targets help students understand what they are supposed to learn in an instructional period and how they will be expected to demonstrate this learning. Figure 6.3 shows sample learning targets that are aligned with a standard and objectives.

---

**CCSS.ELA-Literacy.W.6.2**
Write informative/explanatory texts to examine a topic and convey ideas, concepts, and information through the selection, organization, and analysis of relevant content.

**Lesson Objectives**
These objectives could be for three separate lessons or implemented in the same lesson.

1. After a lesson on the components of writing an effective informational paper, students will be able to utilize a scoring guide to identify the major components in sample informational papers provided by the teacher with 100 percent accuracy.

   • Student learning target: Today, you'll learn about developing an informational paper. By the end of the lesson, you'll be able to identify the important points in several sample papers I'll share with you using a scoring guide.

2. After a lesson on writing informational papers, the students will select a topic and write the introductory paragraph to an informational paper with 100 percent proficiency in utilizing the components of topic selection criteria, clear topic description, and clear topic analysis based on a scoring rubric shared in class.

   • Student learning target: In this lesson, we'll review some important points about informational writing, and then you'll get a chance to show your knowledge by starting an informational paper.

3. Following a review of the essential elements of effective informational papers, students will be able to review and edit an informational introductory paragraph they developed earlier using a scoring rubric shared in a previous class.

   • Student learning target: Yesterday, you wrote the starting paragraph for an informational paper. Today, you get a chance to review your paper and refine and edit it so that it fits the criteria on our scoring guide.

---

*Source for standard: NGA & CCSSO, 2010.*

Figure 6.3: Sample learning targets for a Common Core English language arts standard.

## Writing Objectives and Learning Targets

Now that you know what objectives and learning targets are, it's time to think about writing your own. If you are working in a larger school or department, or if you and your colleagues work together as a professional learning community, you may collaborate on this task to develop department, grade-level, or content-wide lessons and objectives or learning targets. If not, you may be charged with developing your own. When writing objectives and learning targets, you should go through several steps.

1. Review the standards related to your unit or course.

2. Determine the subcomponent (the detailed tasks) of the standard or standards you will be teaching.

3. Decide the exact portion of the standard that you will teach and students will learn during the lesson.

4. Format the objective so that it meets the criteria for objectives. A well-written objective contains four parts:

    a. The students' learning behavior—What the students will do to show or demonstrate their learning

    b. The specific performance required of the students—The exact content or skill to be demonstrated

    c. The conditions under which students will demonstrate the performance—The specific way students will show the learning

    d. The students' level of performance required to be considered successful—The quantitative level to which the student needs to perform to show that he or she has mastered the learning

5. Format the learning target so that it meets the criteria for learning targets. (It describes what students will learn and how they will demonstrate that learning in student-friendly language.)

Figure 6.4 shows the four parts of a learning objective.

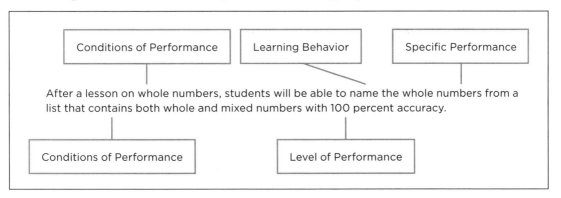

Figure 6.4: Sample learning objective with the four parts labeled.

As you can see from the sample, some parts of an objective can blend together. This can make it a little tricky to identify each part. As a thriving new teacher, you will become proficient in writing learning objectives if you keep these four parts in mind as you develop objectives.

Use the template in the sample in figure 6.5 (page 124) to assist you in developing objectives for your lessons.

**Directions:** Use the following template to help you develop your learning objectives for your classroom. Keep in mind that the learning objectives are designed to guide your work as the teacher.

1. List the standard you will be teaching in this lesson.

   **CCSS.ELA-Literacy.W.6.2**
   Write informative/explanatory texts to examine a topic and convey ideas, concepts, and information through the selection, organization, and analysis of relevant content.

2. List the specific part of the standard you will be focusing on during the lesson.

   This lesson will focus on the subtask of the standard that requires students to use the established scoring to identify the components of topic, major ideas, and information in sample passages. (The process of identification will eventually lead to the students writing their own passages that include these components.)

| Conditions of Performance | Learning Behavior | Specific Performance | Level of Performance |
|---|---|---|---|
| Using an established scoring guide | Identify | Identify major informational components. | 100 percent |

3. List the objective below after putting together all of the parts you have identified:

   After a lesson on the components of writing an effective informational paper, students will be able to utilize a scoring guide to identify the major components in sample informational papers provided by the teacher with 100 percent accuracy.

*Source for standard: NGA & CCSSO, 2010.*

Figure 6.5: Sample plan to develop learning objectives.

*Visit **go.solution-tree.com/instruction** to download a free blank reproducible version of this figure.*

## Planning and Implementing Units

Most thriving new teachers learn very quickly the importance of thoroughly and carefully planning and implementing units of study with their students. A *unit* is a mid- to long-term plan that breaks larger content and process standards into smaller parts. Units typically include student learning outcomes (objectives and learning targets), assessments that will be used to measure student learning, a description of the various lessons to be taught in the unit, the time that is planned for the various aspects of the unit, and resources that will be used in the unit.

Units can be implemented from a few weeks to a few months depending on the complexity of the content being taught. Units may be based on content, academic themes, or other learnings that make sense for the students. Teachers can implement units within one classroom or share their planning among several teachers and classrooms.

To implement a unit effectively, you must plan well. This planning should include considerations for all aspects of the unit. Start by identifying the standard or standards that will be the focus of the unit. A standard could specify the content of the unit, or a standard may focus on a learning *process*. The teacher then determines the content used for learning and practicing the process. Unit planning should also include identification of objectives, outcomes, and learning targets. Finally, the teacher plans details such as assessment, additional resources, unit length, and so on.

A unit may sound complex and difficult to plan, but following a template or process will help you put all of the necessary steps together into a seamless, interesting unit. Figure 6.6 (pages 126–127) is a unit-planning template to assist you in this task.

## Planning Lessons

Thriving new teachers are able to plan and deliver lessons that help students learn topics and content, become and stay engaged, and practice, and then they follow up to ensure student mastery of the lesson content. As a thriving new teacher, consider the following aspects for inclusion in your lessons.

▸ **Warm-up exercise or other activity to engage the students in the learning:** This helps students get into the right mindset for learning and allow students to shift successfully from one lesson to the next.

▸ **Statement of the learning target, purpose, or lesson objective:** It's important to let students know what you are expecting them to learn and be able to do as a result of the lesson.

▸ **Statement of the rationale for the lesson:** Students should understand why they are learning the content in addition to what they are learning.

▸ **Engaging presentation of the information, content, or process to be learned in the lesson:** Be sure students are active participants in the learning and not just passively being presented with the information.

▸ **Checks to ensure that students understand the content or process they learned in the lesson:** If the content of the lesson is what we expect students to learn and later demonstrate, it's crucial to periodically make sure they understand it.

▸ **Opportunities for students to try out or apply the content or processes they learned in the lesson with assistance:** In the first stages of learning, students may feel a little unsure. Provide support for them as they try out the new information they are learning.

▸ **Opportunities for students to apply the content or processes they learned in the lesson on their own:** Finally, it's time for the students to try out the learning on their own. This may include homework assignments, formative assessments, exit slips, and other strategies where students are required to work alone to complete application exercises, or work in small groups practicing what they have learned. The teacher can analyze these formative assessments, independent practices, exit slips, and so on, to make decisions about the next lesson or learning opportunity.

---

**Unit title:** _____

**Unit length:** _____ **Grade level or subject area:** _____

1. Identify the standards addressed in the unit.

2. List the teacher objectives and student learning targets for the unit. Be sure to include objectives and learning targets that address what students will know and be able to do by the end of the unit.

| Objectives for Unit | Student Learning Targets for Unit |
|---|---|
| | |

3. Formative (ongoing) assessments measure student learning growth periodically throughout the unit.
   • Check those you will be using during this unit.
     ☐ Anecdotal records
     ☐ Notes from class discussions
     ☐ Student conferences and individual conversations
     ☐ Quizzes
     ☐ Exit cards
     ☐ Journals, learning logs
     ☐ Performance tasks
     ☐ Individual and group projects
     ☐ Responses to writing prompts
     ☐ Student work portfolios
     ☐ Running records
     ☐ Other

   • How do you plan to use the formative assessment data to make changes to your unit as you implement it?

4. List the various learning strategies and techniques you plan to use to help the students learn and remember the major objectives and learning targets from the unit. Check the major learning methods that you will use throughout this unit.

     ☐ Teacher-developed lecture with periodic student discussion
     ☐ Internet or technology-based information
     ☐ Flipped instruction—students read or view online content, then come to class with questions
     ☐ Reading of information by students
     ☐ Jigsawing articles and information
     ☐ Discussing information in groups
     ☐ Student presentations
     ☐ Student discussion of case studies
     ☐ Student outlining of topic information
     ☐ Students providing written answers to questions
     ☐ Student projects

5. How do you plan to sequence the content, objectives, and the learning targets in this unit?

   a. _____
   b. _____
   c. _____
   d. _____
   e. _____
   f. _____
   g. _____
   h. _____
   i. _____
   j. _____
   k. _____
   l. _____

6. Summative assessments measure student learning growth periodically throughout the unit.

   • Check those you will be using during this unit.

     ☐ Anecdotal records
     ☐ Notes from class discussions
     ☐ Student conferences and individual conversations
     ☐ Chapter or unit test
     ☐ Exit cards
     ☐ Journals, learning logs
     ☐ Performance tasks
     ☐ Individual and group projects
     ☐ Responses to writing prompts
     ☐ Student work portfolios
     ☐ Running records
     ☐ Other

   • How do you plan to use the summative assessment data to make changes to your unit as it is implemented?

7. What are your general impressions of the effectiveness of the unit?

8. What aspects of the unit seemed to go well?

9. What aspects of the unit didn't seem to go well?

10. What will you change the next time you implement this unit?

Figure 6.6: Unit-planning template.

*Visit **go.solution-tree.com/instruction** to download a free reproducible version of this figure.*

Figure 6.7 (page 128) shows a completed lesson-plan template. Some of the same components appear in the lesson-planning tool as in the template for planning a unit (figure 6.6). A lesson is a smaller part of a unit. Since they are so closely related, it makes sense that they share some overlapping components.

**Directions:** Use the following template to plan your lessons.

1. In the following table, develop the objective or objectives you want students to learn in the lesson. After that, convert these objectives into the learning targets you will share with the students.

| Lesson Objective or Objectives | Learning Target or Targets |
|---|---|
| After a lesson on the components of writing an effective informational paper, students will be able to utilize a scoring guide to identify the major components in sample informational papers provided by the teacher with 100 percent accuracy. | Today, you'll learn about developing an informational paper. By the end of the lesson, you'll be able to identify the important points in several sample papers I'll share with you using a scoring guide. |

2. State the introduction or warm-up activity to start the lesson and attract the students to the lesson.

As the students are coming into the classroom, there will be a sample of an informational paper projected on the screen. Students will be asked to review the paper and talk in pairs about why they think it was good. After several students report, I'll say, "How many of you would like to learn how to provide clearer information to those who read your work?" After a few students raise their hands, I'll share the learning target with the students.

3. In the following table, define the content processes you want students to learn in the lesson and how you want them to learn these aspects.

| Content and Processes | Methods for Students to Learn the Content and Processes |
|---|---|
| • I will share the five criteria for good informational papers.<br>• I will share a rubric or scoring guide that contains the five criteria for good informational papers. | • I'll have a listing of the five criteria on the projector. Once I tell the students the five criteria, I'll ask them to talk in small groups about them and their understanding of them.<br>• I'll use the same strategy as above. |

4. List the activities and questions you will ask to help you assess student understanding of the topic and content you have taught them.

I'll listen to the conversations the groups have about the five criteria for effective informational papers. I'll randomly call on students to report on one effective criteria element until all five have been discussed. I'll give them a list of elements and ask them to verbally agree or disagree whether or not the element named is on the original list of five elements I presented in class.

5. List the methods you will use to give the students a chance to practice applying the content and processes they have learned in the lesson.

I'll put the students in groups of three. I'll give each group an informational paper and ask them to identify each element (of the original five) within each paper within their group of three. Once all of the groups have found the elements, I'll have each group share the five elements within each paper.

6. List the activities and assignments you will provide for the students to apply what they have learned in this lesson.

The students will be given two informational papers and asked to identify and mark the five elements of an informational paper in the samples.

Figure 6.7: Lesson-plan template and sample lesson.

*Visit **go.solution-tree.com/instruction** to download a free reproducible blank template of this figure.*

In the sample lesson-plan template, notice the clear and concise descriptors used to define the lesson's elements. You can see how the warm-up activity is aligned to the lesson objective. Also, you can see that although the template asks for details related to each of the learning processes to be implemented, a teacher is free to personalize the activity to meet the intent of these learning processes. Your lesson plan should be useful to you as you consider how you will deliver lessons to your students. Feel free to include more detail if you think you need more specifics in your planning. A thriving new teacher soon learns to plan thoroughly and efficiently to make sure his or her lessons are focused and powerful to help students learn and grow.

## Summary and Reflection

In this chapter, you learned important information about managing the content and curriculum within your teaching concentration. We focused on objectives, learning targets, unit planning, and lesson planning because these are the critical areas for thriving new teachers.

As you reflect on this chapter, please take a few minutes to review the following questions.

▶ Define the term *standard*, and explain why standards are important in your teaching. How can a thriving new teacher use standards to guide his or her planning?

▶ What are the differences between objectives and learning targets? Why are both objectives and learning targets needed in developing a focus in your teaching?

▶ What are some of the key attributes in planning an instructional unit?

▶ Why is it important to include opportunities to verify that students understand the content before sending them off to practice on their own? How can a thriving new teacher ensure students understand the information and processes from a lesson?

If a teacher cannot manage the curriculum, he or she cannot ensure that students will be successful and grow as learners. Improper curriculum management is an area that can get a new teacher into trouble and most likely an area that principals worry about most. You learned the basics in order to get off to a good start and thrive as a new teacher. Once your first year is underway, you may want to spend some time with your mentor, instructional coach, department chair, or others who can help you build on your basic knowledge and implement the curriculum in the manner that is intended by your district.

In the next chapter, you'll learn about the specifics of how to measure your students' learning and your effectiveness as a teacher through sound assessment strategies.

# chapter 7

# Incorporating Assessment

*Jaco, a high school social studies teacher, is implementing a unit on the United States Constitution. In one of the unit lessons, Jaco presents information related to the first five amendments. After the presentation, he has the students meet in small groups and discuss some of the implications of these amendments for today's world. As the student groups meet, Jaco walks around the room and listens to their comments, monitoring their progress.*

*Toward the end of the lesson, Jaco gives each student exit cards. On each card there is a question asking students to briefly summarize what they learned about the amendments. He asks each student to complete his or her exit card and then hand it to him as he or she leaves.*

*After school, Jaco reviews the exit cards and makes note of the students' answers. From his analysis, a majority of the students meets the learning target he has shared with them at the beginning of the lesson. Jaco also notices that a small number of students did not fully understand the content related to the learning target. He knows he has to plan an activity the following day to review the content with these students to ensure they master the learning target. The exit cards help Jaco gather ongoing assessment information to assist in the learning process.*

In this example, we see how Jaco uses an informal formative assessment to gather information about the level of learning that occurs during his lesson. He uses that information to decide how to move forward with those students who understand the concepts while also determining how to help the students who need more time or additional instruction.

To become a thriving new teacher, you will find it is important to understand and be able to implement the basic ideas and strategies related to student assessment. In today's schools, teachers are expected to help their students make gains in learning growth to contribute to the overall growth of the school. During these basic assessment strategies, your work will focus on gathering feedback about student learning to help you see the level of student learning and understanding in relation to your objectives and learning targets. You'll also use assessment to measure your students' academic growth overall toward district and state or national standards through the use of more summative or standardized assessments.

## Assessment Basics

Thriving new teachers understand several considerations related to assessment use in their classrooms. The purpose for assessment is one of its fundamental aspects. Authors Richard Stiggins, Judith Arter, Jan Chappuis, and Stephen Chappuis (2004) refer to two types of assessment: (1) assessment *of* learning and (2) assessment *for* learning.

In assessment *of* learning, the teacher assesses what the students have learned. This type of assessment helps measure the curriculum and the instruction that have taken place during a period of time. In assessment *for* learning, the teacher assesses students to measure their learning and then makes decisions to refine, reteach, or move on based on the assessments' results. In assessments for learning, the teacher is trying to determine the next steps in instruction based on learner need.

Another aspect to consider is what to assess. In looking at what to assess, the teacher should focus on those aspects or indicators that make up the essential learnings of the lesson or unit. These essentials could be foundational or prerequisite skills that students are learning that they will need in future lessons or important, stand-alone skills that they may only get during that unit or lesson.

Finally, teachers need to look at their assessments' timing. In looking at timing, it's important to think about whether you want to assess at the start of a unit or lesson, during a lesson or unit, or at the end of a lesson or unit. Each time frame has advantages to consider. For example, a teacher may want to determine the level of knowledge the students have before the unit begins. Knowing this level will help the teacher decide what to focus on and what to eliminate from instruction. By focusing on the students' exact needs and eliminating extra or unnecessary content, the teacher will be able to spend more time on what's crucial for student success.

In some cases, teachers will want to assess students partway through the lesson or unit to see how and what they are learning. This ongoing assessment will be formative—it will impact the learning. Once you have analyzed the formative assessment results, make changes by reteaching content, presenting it in a different manner, extending and enriching it, and using other strategies depending on the outcome of the assessment. Ongoing or formative assessments help you make midcourse corrections to keep the learning on track.

Assessments that teachers implement at the end of a lesson or unit will determine what essentials students have learned or retained. These are typically called summative assessments. Summative assessments sum up the learning. Some districts have developed common summative assessments that all teachers implement. These assessments help measure the teaching and curriculum's effectiveness. Teachers might give end-of-unit tests, end-of-chapter tests, state summative assessments, and national assessments to measure learning.

This chapter focuses on assessment strategies you can use as a new teacher to shape your instruction and ensure students are meeting learning objectives.

## Preassessment

In chapter 6, we talked about developing a unit plan. Within the unit plan, we mentioned the value of conducting a preassessment before the beginning of a lesson or unit. Conducting a preassessment will help you determine the level of knowledge students have at the beginning of the unit or lesson. Once you have determined each student's starting level of understanding, you need to consider how you will meet your students' needs, such as with differentiation, the use of flexible groupings, curriculum compacting, and other accommodations. You may want to work with your principal, instructional coach, peer coach, mentor, or other support person to determine what strategies and accommodations will best suit your students' needs.

Typically, teachers review the learning objectives that guide the unit and then decide which of these learning objectives they need to assess to determine students' understanding related to the objectives. For the selected learning objectives, teachers design tasks or problems that students answer or solve, thus alerting you whether or not they know and understand the learning objectives.

The level of the learning objective has a large impact on which objectives might be on a preassessment. For example, in examining the curriculum for a subject area or grade level, a teacher might see that three objectives that are part of an upcoming unit are newly introduced in this subject area or grade level. The students might benefit from not being able to "preassess out" of this learning and therefore completing extended instruction on these objectives. On the other hand, a teacher might notice that a particular set of objectives was introduced several years ago and is repeated in other grade levels and subject areas. In this case, the students might benefit from having an opportunity to demonstrate their mastery of these objectives in order to spend more time on other, more difficult objectives. As a new teacher, carefully examine each objective within a unit to determine which ones might be candidates for preassessment opportunities. It might be helpful to seek the counsel of an instructional coach, mentor, peer coach, or other colleague in deciding which objectives might be candidates for preassessment.

In addition to preassessing to understand students' level of need and understanding, teachers also use preassessment to assist in establishing flexible grouping. Many teachers find it beneficial to put students in groups based on their knowledge and skills for particular units. These groupings are normally called *flexible groupings* because the groups will change based on the unit, the skills contained within a unit, and the students' knowledge of the skills within each unit. For example, within a unit, students may be grouped together in several small groups based on their content knowledge and also grouped based on their ability to analyze unit information. Preassessments are helpful in determining initial groupings, and periodic assessments will help to determine if the groups need to be adjusted as the unit is implemented.

Another reason to preassess is to identify potential areas of difficulty before teaching a unit. If a teacher gives a preassessment and the results show that a large percentage of students have significant deficits in several unit or lesson objectives, you will need to spend more time in those areas developing prerequisite skills or in overcoming deficits in the student knowledge base. Conducting a preassessment will help you anticipate and proactively deal with these deficit areas before moving into more complex content.

Assessments can take a variety of forms and use a variety of activities and strategies. The following activities and strategies are commonly implemented in schools. As you review them, think about how they may fit your classroom and teaching.

## KWL Chart

There are many variations to the KWL chart. It typically refers to three aspects of learning: (1) what I already *know*, (2) what I *want* to know, and (3) what I *learned*.

To use KWL, you conduct a short overview of the upcoming unit or lesson. In this overview, provide students with specific information about the objectives, content, some of the learning activities, and other aspects of the unit. Then give students a KWL chart and ask them to complete columns one and two. A blank KWL chart appears in figure 7.1.

| What I Already Know | What I Want to Know | What I Learned |
|---|---|---|
| | | |

Figure 7.1: KWL chart template.

*Visit **go.solution-tree.com/instruction** to download a free reproducible version of this figure.*

Once students complete the KWL chart, you review their comments. If a majority of students reports that they already know certain content you are planning to include in the unit, you may need to reassess the depth of coverage of this concept. A more comprehensive assessment of the material the students say they know is necessary to make sure they truly understand these elements at the end of the lesson or unit. Traditional assessments such as tests, quizzes, student projects, and writing samples can be used to gather information to complete this column.

## KWL Survey

The KWL survey is a strategy we have seen teachers use successfully and is a slight variation of the KWL process discussed in the previous section. In this strategy, the teacher makes a short survey that contains some of the skills and information to be taught in an upcoming unit. Students complete the survey to show what they know about the topic. See figure 7.2 (page 136) for a template for a KWL survey.

Once the students have completed the KWL survey, collect them and analyze the results. These results can be used to plan the areas of concentration within the unit.

| Unit _____ Preassessment _____ | | | |
|---|---|---|---|
| **Student name:** _____ | | | |
| **Directions:** Please rate your knowledge of the content or skills listed in the first column so I understand how much you know about our upcoming unit. For each content area or skill, rate your level of knowledge or interest as *some knowledge*, *extensive knowledge*, or *interested in learning more*. | | | |
| | **Some Knowledge** | **Extensive Knowledge** | **Interested in Learning More** |
| 1. _____<br><br>Student comments or questions: | | | |
| 2. _____<br><br>Student comments or questions: | | | |
| 3. _____<br><br>Student comments or questions: | | | |
| 4. _____<br><br>Student comments or questions: | | | |
| 5. _____<br><br>Student comments or questions: | | | |
| Are there any other content areas or skills that you'd like to explore within this unit that were not addressed in the rating scale above? Please list them here. | | | |

Figure 7.2: KWL survey template.

*Visit go.solution-tree.com/instruction to download a free reproducible version of this figure.*

## KWL Carousel

Another engaging way to find out what students know in advance of starting a unit is to engage them in an active learning strategy called KWL carouseling. This activity is not designed to gather specific individual information. It is a good way to get a total picture of the whole class. The activity works like this.

1. List the major learning targets or objectives you have planned for the upcoming unit on large sheets of chart paper. Each skill or

objective should be listed separately on its own piece of paper. Below each target, write "What We Know" on the left side and "What We'd Like to Learn More About" on the right. This activity works best if you limit the number of charts to eight to ten total. You may want to only focus on a small number of the major learning objectives or learning targets.

2.  Divide the class into smaller groups of four students each.

3.  Assign each group to stand by one of the posted charts and provide each group with a marker.

4.  Ask each group to talk about the topic on their assigned chart and generate ideas for the "What We Know" and "What We'd Like to Learn More About" columns for five minutes. As the students discuss what they already know and what they want to know, one of the group members should write down the ideas generated in the appropriate column. They should leave about one third of the chart empty at the bottom for other students to add their ideas later.

5.  While the groups are talking and writing, walk around the room to listen to the conversations and watch what the students are writing under each heading. You'll want to use your observations later as you analyze what students have written on the charts.

6.  Once you notice that most of the groups have finished their discussion, stop the groups and get their attention. Once you have everyone's attention, provide the following directions:

    • Tell students that in a minute, you're going to play a song. When they hear the music, their entire group should rotate to the next chart that is located to their right.

    • Once groups get to the next chart, they should read the ideas the previous group wrote. Then they should add at least one idea under each heading using their marker.

    • Tell students that when they hear the music again, they should move one more chart to the right. Once they get there they should read the previous ideas and add at least one more under each heading. Tell them to repeat the same process each time the song comes on.

7.  Play some music. When the music comes on, students move one chart clockwise.

8.  Continue the process until students have visited each chart.

When all groups have visited all charts, stop the activity, get students' attention, and hold a conversation with them about their work. Ask the groups to expand or add more detail in relation to their responses. After the students return to their seats, gather up the charts and use them in refining your plan for the upcoming unit. Figure 7.3 shows a sample carouseling chart.

| Content Area I | |
| --- | --- |
| What We Know | What We'd Like to Learn More About |
| | |

Figure 7.3: Sample carouseling chart.

*Visit* **go.solution-tree.com/instruction** *to download a free reproducible version of this figure.*

### Pretesting

In a unit or lesson pretest, students are asked to respond to a representative sample of the types of problems or questions they will encounter during the unit. If they can show their understanding or mastery of the pretest items, the teacher knows they probably understand the content well enough that they won't need to discuss it during the unit.

The number of problems that students complete to demonstrate their learning can vary based on the complexity and difficulty level of the content being pretested. In some cases, students may be asked to only complete a few problems or questions while in other, more complex areas, students may have to address a longer list of problems or questions.

In developing pretests for students, consider consulting your department, other colleagues, your instructional or peer coach, or your mentor. You can also find pretests and pretesting materials in many of the teacher's editions of the textbooks you may be using in your class.

## Assessment During Learning

There are a variety of activities and strategies new teachers can use during instruction to assess where students are in their learning. These are formative assessment strategies because they impact the instruction.

### Exit Tickets or Passes

Exit tickets or passes are a good way to gather data about student learning at the end of a lesson. For this strategy, the teacher poses a question for students at the end of class, handing out slips of paper on which each student can write his or her response to the question. Once the class period has ended, students give their exit tickets or passes to the teacher, who is standing at the door to gather them and dismiss the students from the classroom. These exit tickets or passes are considered the students "tickets out of the classroom." The teacher thanks each student for submitting his or her slip.

The teacher reviews the completed exit tickets or passes to see what the students learned in the lesson. For those students who did learn the content or concepts well, the teacher can move to the next concept. If the students don't know the content well, the teacher can decide to reteach or review the content again during the next opportunity to ensure students will have a chance to learn the concepts.

## Choral Responses

In this formative assessment strategy, the teacher poses a question, then asks all the students to respond at the same time. For example, a teacher might ask the students, "How many senators does each state in the United States have in the Senate?" The teacher could then say, "Answer." The students would then answer the question all together by stating, "Two." The teacher listens for the volume of answers not matching the correct answer. This lets the teacher know if not everyone knows the answer and reteaching might be needed. If the teacher hears most students say the correct answer but the responses did not sound definite or strong, the teacher might also need to reteach the concept.

This activity can be done quickly with little preparation; a teacher can stop and use it at any point in a lesson. However, it's not very scientific, and it may be hard to determine who exactly knows the concept and who does not. You may need to follow up with a more specific or traditional assessment to get more detailed information.

## Group Products and Presentations

For this strategy, teachers break the class into small groups and assign each with a section or part of the lesson's content. They then ask each small group to review its section and then in about ten minutes plan a presentation, skit, song, or other visual that illustrates or helps teach the concepts in the section it reviewed. Tell students this group product will be shared with the remainder of the class to help them learn or review the information. Once each group has had a chance to plan its session, provide about five minutes per group to present its work to the larger group. During their planning time, walk around the room and listen to some of the conversations. You will gain an understanding of what they know or remember.

As the groups are presenting, listen carefully to what they are saying to further assess their understanding of the concepts. After each group presents, ask the students in the audience to share what they learned about the concept. If the students understand the major concepts, it's okay to move on. If there are issues with their understanding, you can reteach them now or come back to the concept tomorrow.

If you need more detailed data on how individual students are performing, you should consider using other assessment instruments.

## Random Question Response

Another simple way to randomly assess student learning is to call on students to answer select questions. Make sure that a representative sample of students answers the questions to ensure that the results you get reflect student understanding. For example, if the students who always answer first are the ones who answer these questions, it may appear that everyone knows the answers when they may not. Similarly, if you only call on the students who normally don't answer in class or always have difficulty in understanding content, you may assume that the entire class is having difficulty.

Following are some methods you can use to randomly select respondents. They include:

▸ Write all the student names on Popsicle sticks (one name per stick), put all the sticks in a container, and then draw one name at a time to answer each question.

▸ Write all students' names on playing cards (one per card), shuffle the deck, and draw one name at a time to answer each question.

▸ Use a computer program or app to randomly select numbers that have been assigned to individual students. When a student's number is selected, that student has to answer the question. You can project the computer screen in the classroom for more excitement.

▸ Assign each student a number, roll one to three dice, and select the number of the student that corresponds to the total of numbers on the dice to answer each question. Vary the number of dice with each roll so lower and higher numbers have a probability of being selected.

▸ Ask each student to write his or her name on a small piece of paper. Put all the pieces of paper in a container and draw one randomly. Ask that student to answer the first question. Repeat the procedure for each of the other questions.

▶ Get a small, soft ball. Pose the first question, and then toss the ball to a student. That student should answer the question and then toss the ball back to you. Pose a second question and follow the same process to select another student. Repeat the process until all the questions have been answered.

## Group Signaling

Group signaling is a process to quickly gather assessment data from a large group all at once. In this strategy, the group simultaneously responds to a question using some sort of signal. The signal should clearly show you whether or not students know the answer to the questions. For example, if a teacher says, "Show me with your fingers whether you think the answer is one, two, or three," the students could show one, two, or three fingers. The teacher will immediately be able to see if students have learned the concept.

You can also use group signaling to verify yes/no or either/or responses. Students can raise their hands for a yes response and keep them down for no. They can raise their hands for choice number one or keep them down for choice number two.

Hand signaling can be used to designate larger/smaller or sooner/later responses. For example, the teacher says, "I'll name two objects, then I'll say them again. You signal which one is larger or smaller with your hands." The students then show the relative size relationships with their hands. The possibilities for group signaling are only limited by your imagination and creativity.

Since some students may want to look at or copy their peers' responses, you could ask students to close their eyes or hold their signal until you tell them to go. Then they all show the signal at the same time, ensuring that they are providing the most accurate assessment of what they think.

## Short Summaries

Another strategy to assess student learning during instruction is to ask students to write a short summary of their knowledge of the lesson or concept in a journal or other document. Give the students a prompt to respond to that is related to the learning target or targets or let them design their own responses. After students have finished writing, collect and review their work looking for key information. This strategy does not take a lot of time to implement, but it can give you some good information about what your students are learning.

## Classroom Polls or Clickers

There is a wide variety of technology-assisted polling and survey programs available for teachers. Some districts offer these for their teachers to use as assessment tools. These programs are a good tool teachers can use to periodically stop the lesson, ask questions of students, and then get their responses immediately to assess their learning. Some programs will even allow you to make a table or graph of the responses. Others actually track who provided each response so you can follow up and provide assistance with students who do not seem to understand the learning targets from the lesson or unit.

As technology continues to evolve, there are always new and exciting tools becoming available for the classroom. Some polling apps for smartphones even let students use their own cell phones to respond to assessment questions.

## Whiteboard Responses

Another successful informal group-response strategy is called whiteboard responses. With this strategy, each student gets a small whiteboard, a dry-erase marker, and a sock. The teacher poses a question then gives the students a short amount of time to write their responses to the question on their boards. Once everyone is finished, the teacher walks around and checks the boards individually or has all of the students share the information on their whiteboards simultaneously.

This strategy is relatively easy to implement and gives teachers good information related to student learning. Teachers can follow up with more formal assessments if necessary.

## Response Cards

Some teachers find that providing students with response cards can be a helpful way for students to signal their responses to questions. These cards can be fairly simple, containing only a few options for responses in some cases, or somewhat complex containing more information that students can use to provide responses.

The students keep these cards either on or inside their desks and use them when answering questions. Students can make these response cards, or teachers can make them. Teachers may also have the response cards laminated so they are more durable for heavy use by students.

During the strategy, pose questions and then ask students to signal their responses or answers. In order to signal their responses, students can simply point to the correct answers on their cards and show them to the teacher. This provides a quick way for the teacher to see who knows the concept (and shows the correct answer) and who does not know the concept (and shows an incorrect answer). Figure 7.4 shows an example of a student-response card.

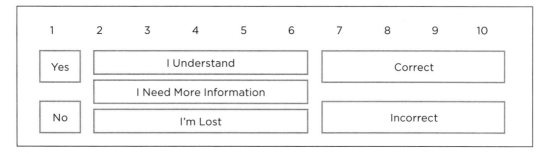

Figure 7.4: Sample student-response card.

*Visit* **go.solution-tree.com/instruction** *to download a free reproducible version of this figure.*

## Color-Coded Feedback

Color-coded feedback is an excellent way to get students to give you some information about their own perceptions of their understanding of concepts or ideas presented in a lesson. The following are the steps for this strategy:

1.  Provide students with written content or notes related to the lesson or unit.

2.  Ask each student to review the notes and mark the areas to show their level of understanding—

    -   Mark areas that you understand clearly with green.
    -   Mark areas that you are somewhat unsure of in yellow.
    -   Mark areas that you are confused by or totally unsure of in red.

3.  Walk around the classroom and review the color coding, looking for trends in the colors you see that students have used to identify their level of understanding.

4.  Decide on your strategy to help students improve their understanding of the red and yellow areas. Decide whether to reteach or review the skill with a small group or with the entire class.

## Sentence Reflectors

At the end of a lesson, ask students to complete the following sentence frames, either orally with a partner or in writing, to reflect on what they learned or still want or need to learn.

▸ Today I learned . . .

▸ Today I wondered . . .

> ▶ Today I practiced . . .

> ▶ Today I felt . . .

> ▶ Today I thought . . .

> ▶ Today I didn't understand . . .

> ▶ Today I understood . . .

> ▶ Today I realized . . .

## Test-Question Generation

A highly effective strategy for assessing learning during instruction is asking students to generate a question that could be used on a future test for the content they have learned in the lesson. Teachers then choose the top test questions. Some questions will appear on the test at the end of the unit. Teachers can include the names of students with their questions, and they can give students automatic credit for a question they designed that appears on the test. These incentives make it even more desirable for students to generate great test questions.

If students can generate test questions, you can be reasonably sure that they understand the content related to the question. Some teachers even require that students provide the correct answer for the question. This further verifies student understanding.

## Information Frenzy

The information frenzy (adapted from Eller & Eller, 2015) is a great activity to use in gathering informal and formative assessment data. It also helps to keep students on track and on task. Use it at the beginning of an instructional period or at the end of a lesson as a review. To conduct this activity:

1. Divide the class into smaller pairs.

2. Within each pair, designate one student as person A and the other as person B.

3. Explain the rest of the process—

   - Each person (A and B) will get a chance to talk uninterrupted about what she or he remembers or finds significant about the topic or previous lesson.

   - In round one, each person will get one and a half minutes to talk without being interrupted or repeating anything the other person says.

   - In round two, each person will get forty-five seconds to talk without being interrupted or repeating anything the other person says.

- In round three, each person will get twenty seconds to talk without being interrupted or repeating anything the other person says.

- After round three, both person A and person B will have about two minutes total to have an informal conversation about any unfinished thought or about the topic in general.

4. Follow this process, calling time in each round so both students have a chance to speak.

5. As students are talking, walk around the room, listening to the student conversations to see what everyone learns and remembers.

The critical aspect of this activity is when the teacher walks around listening to the conversations. Some teachers carry a notebook and record their observations as they listen to the students. Others may hold a debriefing session with the whole class after the activity is over to hear what students say they learned during the activity.

## Question Clarification With Friends

This is another active learning strategy that can be used as an informal assessment. This activity asks small-group members to reach out to others in the class who they think can provide the answers to a series of review questions the teacher generates. It is a good strategy for formative assessment because it focuses on students' abilities to recall information on the topic. It works like this.

1. Divide the class into groups of three. Have them sit together as a team.

2. Within each trio (team), ask the students to designate a letter for each person on the team. There should be a person A, a person B, and a person C.

3. Tell students that you will be showing the entire class a set of three questions. These questions will be designated as question A, question B, and question C. When the questions are shown, each person should only read the question that corresponds to his or her letter. For example, person A should only review question A, person B should only review question B, and person C should only review question C. The goal of team members reviewing the questions at this stage is to confirm they understand what is being asked—not to provide answers.

4. After the students have a chance to review the questions, ask them if they need any clarification on the questions.

5. Once all information for each question has been clarified, tell the entire group that its task will be for members to leave their small group and find someone else in the room who they think can answer the question that corresponds to their letter. This other person can be anyone in the room except someone from their own small group. Tell students you will give them a signal when they are to start finding the other person to answer their question.

6. Once you give the signal to start, students should walk around the room looking for someone else who can answer their assigned question. They ask the other student the question and then write down the response. The second student (the one who provides the answer for the first student) can ask the first student for an answer to his or her question or move on to another student.

7. After it is evident that everyone has an answer to his or her question, end this part of the activity and ask each student to return to his or her small trio group.

8. Once the students are all back in their trios, person A, B, and C each gets a chance to report the answer she or he gathered during the previous step.

9. After each person reports the answer to his or her question to the group, that group will discuss the accuracy of the answer and make changes to it until the group agrees on it.

10. After the groups have all had a chance to discuss their answers, hold an informal conversation with the entire class. During this discussion, you can determine what students have learned about the concept.

This active learning activity is an excellent way to get informal assessment information from students, especially if you are able to walk around and listen to students as they are talking about their questions.

### Wander Around Review

This activity can be both fun to do and informative for teachers gathering formative assessment data. The following explains how the activity works.

1. Explain to students that you will be doing a review activity involving music and discussions.

2. Tell students that you will be playing music, and while the music is playing, they need to wander around the classroom in a random manner.

3. When the music stops, the students should stop and find a partner.

4. Once they find a partner, you should pose a review question and ask the students to talk with their partner about it. They should talk about the question for one to two minutes until the music starts again.

5. Once the music starts again, have the students resume wandering around. When the music stops, the students find a new partner.

6. Once the students find a new partner, pose another question for the students to discuss.

7. Continue the process in the same format for several more rounds.

8. Hold a conversation at the conclusion of the activity about what students discussed during the activity.

This activity is designed to gather general assessment information. If you want more specific assessment information about particular students or learning targets, you may need to administer a more formal or traditional assessment.

## Assessment After Learning

Much of the information in this chapter focuses on formative assessment. Formative assessment provides a teacher with information to make decisions on a day-to-day, week-to-week basis. It helps a teacher make instructional decisions and mid-course corrections to help students grow and learn.

At some point, a teacher wants to find out how students did on a larger, more comprehensive scale. This is called *summative assessment*. Summative assessments are more final in scope and help a teacher determine what students have learned over an extended period of time. Following are several examples of summative assessments (Eller & Eller, 2015).

▸ **Locally developed assessments:** Locally developed assessments can provide periodic measures of student learning. These assessments may be more closely aligned to the district curriculum and priorities and can be administered multiple times during a year or evaluation cycle. This frequency can help administrators work with teachers in coaching situations.

▸ **Unit or chapter tests:** Unit or chapter assessments can be used periodically during an evaluation cycle. They have the potential to be more focused on the unique or specialized curricula being implemented in the district. However, unit or chapter tests do present some difficulties. Since they are typically designed by the teacher, they may have biases, design flaws, and so on. Even with these difficulties, unit or chapter tests can be a good source of data.

▸ **Quizzes:** Quizzes provide an opportunity for teachers to look at student achievement on an even more regular basis. However, they can present difficulties similar to those of unit or chapter tests.

▸ **Student work products and projects:** Because student work products and projects give an ongoing picture of student knowledge, they can help educators examine regular trends in student learning. When using student products and projects to assess student learning, keep in mind that they are subject to the biases of those assessing.

In many districts, teachers in the same grade levels or academic areas use similar summative assessment tools. Check with your principal, mentor, peer coach, or colleagues to obtain the common summative assessments you should use with your students.

## Summary and Reflection

In this chapter, we learned about the different kinds of assessment and examined some preassessment strategies and formative assessment strategies new teachers can use in the classroom to assess student learning. As you reflect on the information in this chapter, answer the following questions.

▸ What are assessments' purposes?

▸ How can teachers use preassessments to determine the focus areas for upcoming units?

▸ What are some strategies that can be helpful in conducting formative assessments? What does the teacher need to consider when using active learning strategies for assessment purposes?

In the next chapter, we'll look at teaching strategies designed to engage students that will be helpful for thriving new teachers to consider.

# chapter 8
# Engaging Students in the Classroom

*Liam, a new elementary school teacher, is preparing to teach a unit on measurement to his fifth-grade class. As he looks through the mathematics series the district uses, he finds a lot of information about teaching measurement units but not a lot of interesting activities. He knows that it is important for students to understand the various units of measurement but also knows that they need to have a hands-on experience with this content.*

*Liam asks his instructional coach, Jennifer, about some ideas he could use to introduce the measurement unit. Jennifer says that she has some large tape-measuring strips that Liam can use to have the students measure various items on the playground. Jennifer says other teachers have used this activity in the past and find it helpful in introducing the idea of measurement units.*

*Liam introduces his unit by asking students to share opportunities where they have measured items in the past. Only a few students have stories to share so Liam asks them, "How many of you would like to measure some items on our playground?" All of the students enthusiastically raise their hands. Liam takes some time to introduce the students to the large tape measures and discusses the process for using them on the playground. He divides the students into teams of three and assigns roles to each team member. Each team is told to measure three items and bring back the measurements to the class.*

*When the students return, each trio reports its results, and Liam helps each team design a graph to represent these results. On the exit card Liam uses to assess what the students learned in the lesson, the students answer his prompt correctly. The lesson is a success in launching his unit on measurement!*

In the example, Liam went beyond just presenting information from the mathematics book so his students could experience a hands-on introduction to the concept of measurement. He worked with his instructional coach to get ideas to make the learning more engaging. Liam made sure the activity would help his students meet their learning objectives for the beginning of the unit. Liam identified the major procedures necessary for success in the activity and took the time to review them with students before starting. Students were on task and well-behaved even though he took them to the playground. Because of his planning, the lesson was a success.

Thriving new teachers use a variety of teaching strategies to ensure their units and lessons are engaging and effective. Teaching strategies help students process and learn the information in an engaging way. In this chapter, we will introduce you to many teaching strategies to help you make your lessons more engaging and increase active learning and student success.

## Active Student Engagement in Learning

While there are many ways to think about student involvement, two common terms used in education are student engagement and active learning. Authors Chet Meyers and Thomas B. Jones (1993) define *active learning* as when students are able to:

> Talk and listen, read, write, and reflect as they approach course content through problem-solving exercises, informal small groups, simulations, case studies, role playing, and other activities—all of which require students to apply what they are learning. (p. xi)

Researchers have advocated for an increase in student involvement in their own learning. Author John Hattie (2012) has completed a series of meta-analyses related to teaching strategies. While some of the results focus on teacher-based strategies (for example, teacher relationships and teacher clarity), results for active learning or active engagement (for example, discussion, metacognition, and so on) showed a high connection to improving student achievement. When students are engaged in their learning, they have a higher level of investment and involvement. They move from being passive learners to being more connected to the learning.

Although there are times when lecturing can be an appropriate method for disseminating information, researchers like Hattie (2012) suggest that using a variety of instructional strategies can positively enhance student learning. Obviously, teaching strategies should be carefully matched to the teaching objectives of a particular lesson.

As you get ready to select teaching strategies to use in a lesson or unit, consider some of the questions figure 8.1 outlines.

---

1. What are the learning objectives and targets that students are expected to master in this lesson or unit?

2. What teaching strategies seem to match the lesson or unit objectives?

3. What strategies match my teaching style or preferences?

4. What strategies will work within the learning culture of my classroom?

5. What strategies will match the way my students like to learn?

---

Figure 8.1: Questions to consider when selecting teaching strategies.

*Visit **go.solution-tree.com/instruction** to download a free reproducible version of this figure.*

The answers to these questions will help you reflect as you select teaching strategies. You may want to also consider other factors such as:

▸ Room size and configuration

▸ Availability of special materials (for example, chart paper and markers)

▸ How other teachers in the building teach—If you are teaching in a markedly unique and different manner than all of the other teachers in the building, it may take some time for students to become accustomed to your methods. Also, you may encounter some negative peer pressure. Keep these points in mind so you are not surprised if you encounter difficulties.

▸ Support of your principal and administrator—This is important because if your principal does not think positively about your strategy, you may encounter difficulty if you are not successful with your implementation.

All these factors will help you select the best strategies to help your students learn the objectives while you also actively engage them in the learning.

## Active Engagement Strategies

If you want to use teaching strategies that actively engage students in your lessons, start at the beginning of the lesson and provide engaging strategies throughout. This section explores techniques that thriving new teachers use from the beginning to the end of their lessons.

### Activities for When Students Enter the Classroom

Once you have greeted students entering the classroom, conduct an opening activity so work starts right away. This helps start class in a positive manner, keeps students on task, and immediately engages them in learning. Some examples of possible topics include:

▸ Ask students to answer a question of the day that is related to the lesson or something that is motivational. A question might focus on a topic in the assigned reading, for example, or on a compelling current event.

▸ Think about the background knowledge needed for the upcoming lesson. Ask students to define one aspect of background for the lesson. For example, a lesson on the subtraction of fractions may require that students use the numerator/denominator relationship. A teacher could list several regular and irregular fractions, asking the students to rename them identifying the numerators and denominators.

▸ Ask students to review a concept from a previous lesson or unit that you want to make sure they remember on a long-term basis. Ask them to provide a definition or illustration of the concept.

After students enter the classroom, give them three to four minutes to answer the posted question. Then they can share their answers with the larger group, meet in pairs to discuss their answers, use signal or response cards to give their answers, show you their answer as you walk around the classroom, or respond in some other way that lets you know what they learned during the activity.

## Activities During the Lesson

Providing active engagement during the lesson helps students engage with the content to reach the learning target. This section presents a variety of possible teaching strategies to use at various stages during the lesson. When you are designing your lessons, select the strategies you feel are the most pertinent based on the material you are teaching, your instructional style and preferences, your students' learning preferences, and the other factors you reflected on in figure 8.1 (page 151). Most of the strategies can be implemented in a variety of classrooms in various grade levels. In the heading for each activity, we provide the grade levels we consider optimal for each activity.

### Acting Out a Story (All Grade Levels)

This strategy uses physical movement to demonstrate and improve comprehension. Break students into small groups of three to four. Assign each group a story or section of content and ask each group to act it out. Students spend three to four minutes planning, and then they present to the other group. After the acting, ask the group to talk about the story or content presented.

A related strategy is to present a section of the story, then stop and ask all of the students to simultaneously demonstrate or act out the section. For example, a teacher might be reading a story where the main character is frightened. The teacher could stop and say, "Show me what Mary's face would look like when she saw the bear walking around her cabin." The students stop and demonstrate the look on Mary's face.

### Recording Books (Primary and Intermediate Elementary)

For students who are auditory learners, consider making digital recordings of books. By providing an audio version of a textbook chapter, storybook, novel, or some other printed material, you help students learn more than if they were just required to read material. Students can use this material independently or in learning centers. These recorded books can be stored electronically and made available on the school's or teacher's website.

### Journaling (Intermediate Elementary Through High School)

Journal writing is a positive and productive way to get students engaged in the learning. An added bonus is that you can get to know your students on a more personal level. Thriving new teachers implement journaling in various ways. You can ask students to keep handwritten journals, record their spoken thoughts, or keep electronic journals in the form of a blog, to name a few. No matter what method you use, the process will help students express themselves and improve their writing and speaking skills.

Most teachers ask students to respond to a writing prompt to start the journaling process. Figure 8.2 shows some examples of writing prompts.

1. If you could start school over again, what would you do differently?
2. What is your favorite part of your day?
3. How do you celebrate events in your life?
4. When was the last time you tried something new, and what was the new thing you tried?
5. If you don't understand something, what do you do?
6. How would you describe yourself in ten words?
7. If your entire life was a movie, what title would best fit?
8. If you could send a message to the entire school, what would you say?
9. If you had the opportunity to teach someone one thing, what would you teach and to whom?

Figure 8.2: Sample writing prompts.

Continued ➡

10. What makes you smile?

11. What drives you to do better at something?

12. What do you really love to do? Do you do it often?

13. What can you do today that you couldn't do a year ago? What are you hoping you can do one year from now?

14. What do you want most out of life?

15. If you could go back in time once and change a single thing, what would it be?

16. If you could ask for one wish, what would it be?

17. When you think of your home, what immediately comes to your mind?

18. How do you spend the majority of your free time? Why?

19. What are you looking forward to?

20. What terrifies you the most?

21. Where would you like to live?

22. What have you done that you're most proud to have achieved?

23. What is your greatest strength? What is something you are working on that you want to improve?

24. What did you do yesterday to make someone's life better?

25. What will you do today that makes someone's life better?

26. What makes you special?

27. What bad habits do you want to break, and why?

28. Would you risk your reputation by standing up for what is right in front of your peers?

29. What are things that stand between you and complete happiness?

*Visit* **go.solution-tree.com/instruction** *to download a free reproducible version of this figure.*

You can adapt the questions for various grade levels and content areas as needed. If you are working with younger students, students with limited background knowledge, or students who are struggling to learn how to read, you can simplify the prompts in figure 8.2. For example, the prompt that says, "What drives you to do better at something?" could be changed to "How do you get better in school?" Think about your students and the kinds of prompts they could understand and use in their writing. Some age groups can read a prompt from a white board or computer projector. Others might need the prompt spoken to them. Use the knowledge you have gained about your students to design the most appropriate prompts and the best ways to deliver them.

Normally, teachers give students about five to ten minutes to write in their journals. This seems to be enough time for students to get a good start with their thoughts.

*Learning Logs (Intermediate Elementary Through High School)*

Learning logs are a simple and straightforward way to help students integrate content and process and express their personal feelings. The strategy is somewhat similar to learning journals, but a learning log is focused only on what the student has learned in a particular lesson or unit. Learning logs are especially powerful for developing metacognitive-processing skills; learning logs support students' capacity to learn from writing rather than writing what they have learned. Metacognition is one of the most productive teaching strategies reported in Hattie's (2012) work.

A common application of learning logs is to have students make entries in their logs during the last five minutes of class. Students can sum up their learning in these short but frequent end-of-class writing exercises. An added benefit of asking students to write at the end of a class session is that it helps with classroom management by keeping students engaged in the last few minutes of class, which are commonly underutilized.

To stimulate student thinking, provide students with question stems posted in the room or in the back of their log books. The following types of stems are useful starting points for the learning log process.

▸ What are three to four things I learned in class today?

▸ After today's lesson, what am I still wondering about?

▸ What did I enjoy in class today?

▸ What things did I find difficult or not enjoyable in class today?

▸ What strategies did my teacher use that helped to support my learning?

▸ What did I contribute to my own and others' learning today?

▸ What can I do in the future to learn more in this class?

Another option is to write four or five key words on the board based on the day's lesson. Ask students to free write about the words for several minutes.

You can collect the logs from time to time to read them and share your written comments with students. This helps build stronger relationships between student and teacher and provides an excellent way to informally assess how well the class is doing.

*Brainstorming (All Grade Levels)*

Brainstorming is widely used in schools to encourage participants to generate ideas. Brainstorming encourages students to participate actively in idea-generation exercises and experience benefits of a multidimensional approach to analyzing problems or solutions.

You can implement the brainstorming technique in a variety of ways.

1. **Structured approach:** First, give the whole class a topic to discuss. Then call on one student at a time to contribute an idea. You can move around the room until everyone has had a chance to share an idea. The advantage of this method is that all students participate and the more vocal students tend not to dominate the discussions. The disadvantage is that the discussions usually do not flow freely as in an unstructured session, and this can make some students feel pressured and uncomfortable.

2. **Unstructured approach:** Allow students to contribute ideas as they think of them. This approach allows for a freer flow of ideas and a more relaxed environment. The drawbacks to this approach are that it can lead to the students not responding at all or to a few students dominating the discussions.

3. **Group approach:** This is a structured approach except that the class is broken into small groups and each group presents its ideas after an allotted amount of time. The advantage of this method is that the students are likely to be more at ease and willing to express their ideas. This also promotes synergy and communication among the students. One drawback to this method is that it is more time intensive than the other two methods.

*Periodic Processing (Intermediate Elementary Through High School)*

One activity to engage students during a lecture is called periodic processing. In this strategy, present information to the students for a designated amount of time (ten minutes). After the designated amount of time is up, students get time (two minutes) to process the information. During the processing time, students can work independently or with a partner or in teams and share what they have learned. The processing time allows students to ask their partner questions about the new learning and clarify concepts. While students are working independently or in groups, circulate the room listening to the discussions. Take notes on what the students know and what they need help with.

*Shoulder or Elbow Partners (All Grade Levels)*

If you want to have students discuss with a partner what they have just learned, have them sit in a circle and ask them to turn to the person whose shoulder is next to their right shoulder to share or discuss the following:

▸ What they have learned so far about the topic

▸ What questions they have or what they don't understand about the topic

After you've given the students a minute or two to discuss with their partner, ask them to share some details related to their conversations. A variation of this activity is to have students talk with the person who is sitting next to their right elbow.

### Aha! Moments (All Grade Levels)

Ask students to write an insight, idea, or a new piece of information they learned during the lesson (their aha! moment). Then have them share their aha moment with a partner. If students are sitting in groups of three or more, ask them to share their aha moment with the students in their group. One person from each group could share the moments with the entire class. This gives students an opportunity to learn from their classmates while keeping them actively engaged in the learning.

### Fish Bowl (Secondary)

For this strategy, you have to arrange the classroom into two circles. Place eight desks in the inner circle and place the remainder of the desks in the outer circle. (The number of desks can vary depending on the class size.) You may want to assign the students their seats. Begin the lesson by explaining the two circles' roles.

▸ **Inner circle:** Students seated in the inner circle discuss a question you will ask the students. Students need to be respectful of each other, listen carefully to each other's answers, and share their thoughts. You can let students discuss or debate an issue as long as you like.

▸ **Outer circle:** Students in the outer circle need to listen carefully to the students in the inner circle and take notes. If a student in the outer circle would like to make a comment or join the discussion, he or she walks up to the inner circle and taps a student on the shoulder. Once a student from the inner circle is tapped on the shoulder, he or she moves to the outer circle and sits in an empty desk. Now a new student has joined the inner circle. This student can add to the discussion.

This is a great strategy to use during language arts or reading time, or after reading several chapters of a novel or the end of a novel. Prepare several questions that require students to think and reflect on the material.

### Jigsaw Reading (Secondary)

Divide a reading assignment into short sections. Assign students to groups of four. Ask each student in the group to take a different short section to read, so that someone in each group is reading each section. After reading, students then take turns explaining their section to their small group. Alternately, ask students who read the same section to meet as a group to discuss the section, and then have the groups present their section to the class.

### Gallery Walk (All Grade Levels)

Place students in groups and ask them to create a poster or symbolic representation of a lesson concept. Once these posters are completed, play music and allow students to wander from poster to poster, reviewing the work, taking notes, or discussing the work in small groups until all students have viewed all posters. After students have completed the gallery walk, stop the music and ask students to stop at their last chart. Have a class discussion about what they learned during the walk.

When introducing this activity to your students, let them know that they will be conducting the gallery walk in place of seat-time activities. Remind them to keep moving and stay on task during the entire time the music is playing. When students are walking around and discussing the information on the charts, watch them and listen to their comments. Listening will help you determine what they are learning during the activity and what you may need to reteach or stress during a follow-up lesson or activity.

### Graffiti Writing (All Grade Levels)

Divide the class into groups of six or less. Then write different topics that the students are learning about at the top of six pieces of chart paper and either tape the paper to the wall or place the chart paper on tables. Provide students with markers, colored pencils, crayons, or pens. Have the students in each group writing or drawing illustrations about the topic on their paper at the same time until you give the class the signal to stop working. Have the group talk about what they wrote or drew about the topic. If you'd like, you can ask the class to conduct one of the other activities discussed previously, such as a gallery walk or the carouseling activity, to share and get feedback about their work.

### Word Walls (All Grade Levels)

A word wall—a wall of words that the students are studying and learning—doesn't have to be a static element of the classroom. Most teachers either write the words on large sticky notes or pieces of paper they tape on the wall. Some teachers cover the entire wall with large sheets of bulletin board paper and then write the words on the paper. Others ask students or groups of students to write the words.

The key to a successful word wall is to make it interactive by using activities that expand the students' understanding of the words and give them practice using them in context. For example, you can ask students to walk around the word wall in pairs and discuss the words they know well and the words they are still learning. Another strategy is to take a picture of the word wall and post it on your website and then ask students to review it and share it with their parents or family members.

When putting up a word wall, make the words big enough so the students can read them. If you are going to ask students to read the words or write on the word wall, make sure to post the paper at the proper height.

### Speed Pairing (Intermediate Elementary Through High School)

Create space in your room for a circle. Have students count off by A and B. The A students create a circle, facing out with space in between each student. Then B students create a circle around them, facing in toward the inner circle.

Provide students with a question from the lesson. Ask the students in group A to share their answers with the student directly facing them from group B. After a minute, ask the group B students to add detail to the answer that the A students gave. Once you feel everyone is done sharing, get the attention of the groups by using a signal.

Then ask the outer circle to move one person to the left while the inner circle stays in their place. Now the students should have a new partner. Provide a new question to the group and repeat the exercise.

### Musical Chairs and Moving With Music (All Grade Levels)

This activity is just like the game musical chairs. For elementary students, ask students to bring their chairs to the circle, and then you remove one chair. Ask students to bring a poem they wrote or any short writing exercise. Begin playing music, and once the music stops, students sit down. The student left standing shares his or her poem or writing with the class. Repeat the exercise as many times as you want.

For secondary students, ask students to move about the room with a writing assignment, such as a poem, an exercise, or even an outline of their writing assignment. You play music, and once the music stops, students share their work with the nearest person. Students also give each other feedback on their writing or their outline. This activity shows students how to give specific feedback and helps them improve their writing skills.

### Vote by Moving (All Grade Levels)

You can use this activity when you have the occasion to share information, mathematics problems, or any answers to questions or problems in class. If the students agree with the answer or concept you present, they stand on the right side of the room. If they disagree, they stand on the left. You can use music for when students are moving around the room, and when it stops, students need to be standing in place. Once all the students are in place, call on a student to explain why he or she agreed or disagreed with the teacher answer or concept. This holds students accountable for their answers.

### Phone a Classmate and 50/50 (Intermediate Elementary Through High School)

Many of you have probably watched the television show *Who Wants to Be a Millionaire*. On the show, if a contestant does not know the answer to a question, he or she can call a friend. You can use this same technique with students. If a student doesn't know an answer to a question during a class discussion, the student may choose to "phone a classmate" to get the answer. The student must ask permission to phone a classmate. The student forms a telephone with his or her thumb and pinky, and then calls the classmate and asks the question. The student listens to the classmate's answer, contemplates its accuracy, and then repeats the answer to the teacher.

Another idea from *Who Wants to Be a Millionaire* is for students who do not know an answer to a question during discussion to request a 50/50 from the teacher. You give the student two answers, one right answer and one wrong answer. The student chooses an answer and explains why it is correct or uses it in a complete sentence if the answer is a vocabulary word, for example.

### Walk Through the Book and Book Scavenger Hunt (Intermediate Elementary Through High School)

Provide an overview for students when introducing a new book or textbook. Some teachers refer to this process as "walking students through" a book to familiarize them with the book's format, pointing out pieces, such as the table of contents, glossaries, maps, index, headings, bold words, and so on. As you walk them through, make sure to occasionally stop and let them interact in small groups about the book. Another excellent way for students to discover parts of books is to do a book scavenger hunt. Provide students with a list of important parts of the book and have them work with a partner to find all the items on the list.

### Zig-Zag Line (Intermediate Elementary Through High School)

This strategy is a great way to get students moving and sharing what they have learned. Students can share from an in-class assignment or homework assignment (for example, a mathematics problem, vocabulary words, concepts from a history unit, and so on). To implement this activity, divide the class into two smaller but equal groups. Then have the groups line up single file so students are facing each other.

Designate one line as line A and the other line as line B. Have the students in line A go first and share their information with the student across from them in line B. Then the partner in line B shares his or her information with the person in line A.

After both partners have shared, have the students in line A move one position to the left. Because of this action, one person in line A will not have a partner and should "peel off" and go line up across from the student at the end of line B who does not have a partner. You can make the activity more fun by playing music each time line A moves to the left and the first person peels off to join the end of line B.

### Topic Search (Intermediate Elementary Through High School)

When you are asking students to complete a research paper on a specific topic, sometimes students have difficulty getting started. Assign students to small groups of six students or fewer. Each student brings to the group his or her topic that the group will be researching. Have students write their topics at the top of a piece of paper. Explain to students that they will be helping their classmates generate ideas for their research topics. When you give the signal, students pass their papers clockwise to the student next to them. The students list as many ideas about the topic as possible. Give the students about a minute to think of ideas to write down. After a minute, ask the students to again pass their papers clockwise to the next students. This continues until each student receives his or her original paper back. Students then study the list their classmates generated, circling the items they would like more information or clarification on. The students take turns in their groups asking questions about the items other students generated. Now students have a lot more ideas to begin their research papers.

## Internet Resources

There are many Internet resources available for teachers to use to find engaging strategies and tools to use with students during instruction. The following sections show just a few of our favorite resources. These resources can be implemented in a variety of grade levels.

### Sheppard Software

Sheppard Software (www.sheppardsoftware.com) has hundreds of free educational games for students. The site has many subjects—geography, mathematics, animals, and science, to name a few—and is organized into many levels for use with a variety of learners.

### PurposeGames

PurposeGames (www.purposegames.com) is a site where teachers can design their own maps, quizzes, and knowledge games to fit their content area and the needs of their students. Personalized resources can be highly motivating for students.

### Quizlet

Quizlet (www.quizlet.com) is an interactive website that is a valuable resource for building content-specific vocabulary and general study skills. Quizlet has flashcards, games, and quizzes. With six different activities, students can study on their own, compete for high scores, and test themselves.

### Pear Deck

Pear Deck (www.peardeck.com) allows you to create interactive, engaging slide presentations to use in your classroom, and it has built-in formative assessment tools. A Google Drive app, it is easy to use and allows for assessments in real time.

### Socrative

Socrative (www.socrative.com) lets you engage and assess your students with educational activities on tablets, laptops, and smartphones. Through the use of real-time questioning and instant result aggregation and visualization, you can gauge the whole class's current level of understanding. Socrative saves teachers time so the class can further collaborate, discuss, extend, and grow as a community of learners. Socrative lets you create student-paced online quizzes that are graded and give students immediate feedback.

### DocentEDU

DocentEDU (www.docentedu.com) turns any website or teacher-created Google document, slideshow, and so on into a student-paced online assignment with embedded questions, polls, links to relevant resources, topics for whole-class discussions, and so on.

### Kahoot!

Kahoot! (https://getkahoot.com) is a web-based student-response program. You can create quizzes, discussion questions, or surveys for your students. Students can use clickers, iPads, iPhones, or notebooks to respond to your questions. It is a platform for asking questions in any subject, language, ability level, or setting, and it assesses how students are doing on a specific topic. It provides the student and teacher with immediate feedback.

## Grouping Strategies

Since students are often divided into smaller groups when teachers implement engaging strategies, we have included this section that contains quick, random ways of regrouping students.

### Birthday Line-Up

This is a good strategy to randomly subdivide the larger group into smaller groups. It is also an energizing activity because the students will be standing up and moving around the room. The following explains how the activity works.

1.  Tell the students that you will be having them line up side by side according to their birth month and day.

2.  Let the students know that the line will start in the front of the room with January and end in the back of the room with December.

3.  Tell the students that they cannot use any verbal communication to let others know their birth month and year.

4.  Once the students have completed the lineup, have them state their birth month and day in order. If a student is out of the birth month and day order, ask her or him to get in the proper order.

5.  Count off students into smaller groups based on the size of the groups you want. If there are twenty-five students, you want them in groups of five, so count them off by fives.

The birthday line-up is a fun activity that will help you to assign smaller groups in a more random manner.

### Clock Partners

Clock partners is a fun, visual way to divide students into pair or partner groupings. The following directions provide instructions for how to implement clock partners:

1.  Provide students with a copy of the clock face from figure 8.3 on page 164.

2.  Ask students to walk around the room and find a partner to fill in on each hour of the clock. At the end of the activity, students will have made twelve different clock partners.

3.  Ask students to keep their clock partner sheet in their desk or notebook. Let them know that they will be using this sheet to form pair groups in later lessons. You will announce a time, and students will then find the partner who is listed for that time on their sheet.

Figure 8.3: Clock-partners template.

*Visit **go.solution-tree.com/instruction** to download a free reproducible version of this figure.*

## Direction Partners: North, South, East, and West

This is similar to the clock-partnering strategy. Provide students with a piece of paper that has North, South, East, and West written on it, and ask them to find a student to be their partner for each direction. Figure 8.4 shows an example of a template for direction partners.

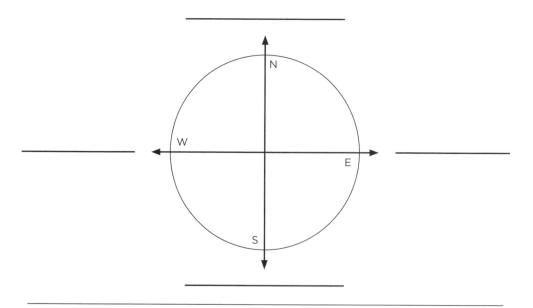

Figure 8.4: Direction-partners template.

*Visit **go.solution-tree.com/instruction** to download a free reproducible version of this figure.*

## Card Groups

Another way to divide students into random groups is to use playing cards. For this strategy, determine your desired group size and then sort the cards so they'll match the group size. For example, if you have twenty students and you want to have groups of four, you would include all four suits of aces through fives. If you wanted to have groups of five you might include cards of all four suits of aces plus include some deuces and jacks as wild cards.

Once you determine the proper number of groups, shuffle the cards and hand them to students. Tell the students you want them to find the other people in the room who have the same type of card (number or suit) and form a group with these students. If you try to form groups larger than four, you will need to have students find the four cards that have the same number, and then ask those students with the wild cards to evenly join the existing groups so that each group contains the desired number of members. For example, let's say you want to form groups of five. You could say, "All of you please find the other people in the room who have the same card as you *except* if you are holding a deuce or joker. Those students should wait and join one of the groups once they have four members. Each one of you holding a deuce or joker should join one of the existing groups of four."

Using cards can be an effective way to randomly regroup students. You can also make the process more purposeful by "stacking the deck" so that certain students receive certain cards. Stacking the deck gives the appearance of random group selection while making sure certain students get assigned to certain groups.

## Sticker Groups

Placing stickers on the backs of handouts, nametags, and other instructional materials is an additional good way to divide students into smaller, more randomized groups. Similar to the card group strategy, you have to first determine how many groups you will have and how many students will be in each group. Once this is determined, you can count out the proper numbers of corresponding stickers and then randomly place them on the handouts or other instructional materials. When the students get the handouts or materials, ask them to look on the back, find the sticker, and find the other people in the group who have similar stickers.

There will be a little noise as the students move from their seats to their new groups. If you have taught students how to move around the room (a student behavior discussed previously in this book), they should be able to complete the move quickly.

### Candy Bar Groups

This strategy is similar to others we have presented except that candy bar types are used to divide the students into groups. As with the other strategies in this section, teachers will need to determine the size and number of groups they desire before starting the activity.

Once the number and group size are determined, the teacher selects the appropriate number and variety of candy bars and places them in a bucket. The fun-size bars are the best candy to use since they are smaller and less expensive than full-sized bars. If the teacher wants to have six groups each containing four students, she would sort out six different candy bar varieties and include four of each variety in the bucket. The teacher then walks around with the bucket and asks each student to select one bar.

Once every student has selected a bar, the teacher asks the students to form groups with others who have the same candy bar. Once groups have formed, students can eat their bars (or wait until the activity is over, if the teacher prefers).

### Paper Color Groups

Another way to group students is to make copies of handouts or materials in different colors. Just like the other activities we have discussed in this section, you must start by thinking about the number of groups and students in each group first. Select the number of colors to correspond to the number of groups. The number of copies of each color should correspond to the number of students in each group. Once the copies are made, shuffle the packets or handouts so the colors are arranged in a random manner. Ask the students to form new groups making sure they are grouped with students who have the same color handout as they have. Once the new groups have formed, provide them with details related to their group task.

### Shoe Size Groups

In this strategy, ask students to group themselves according to similar shoe sizes. Depending on the grade level you teach, there might not be much variation in student shoe size. If you think it might be hard to develop groupings, consider grouping based on size ranges. Or, if you would like to increase the diversity of the group, have students organize themselves so that their group contains a variety of shoe sizes.

Use your discretion in implementing this strategy if you think some students may be teased for having an unusually large or small shoe size.

## Height Groups

Another fun way to break the class into smaller groups is to use height. In order to implement this idea, ask students to line up side by side based on their height (either tallest to shortest or shortest to tallest). Then have the students count off (for example, 1, 2, 3, 1, 2, 3 . . .) so they can form groups based on their number (1, 2, or 3). A variation on this activity is for the teacher to clump students into groups based on similar heights (for example, put the first three students in one group, the next three in another, and so on).

As in the foot size activity, be careful using this in some classroom settings if you think students may be sensitive about their height and subject to teasing.

## Summary and Reflection

In this chapter, we have presented a sampling of highly effective instructional strategies that thriving new teachers find to be helpful and effective in working with students. As you review the information you've learned in this chapter, please take a few minutes to reflect on the following questions.

▸ Why is it important to engage students in the content of your unit or lessons?

▸ How can dividing students into smaller groups help to increase their involvement and engagement in lessons?

▸ What are some grouping and engagement activities that will work in your classroom and fit your teaching style?

▸ How does brainstorming help to bring out creativity in students?

▸ What are some instructional strategies you found in this chapter that you feel might be helpful to you in your teaching?

Now that we have examined some instructional strategies, it's time to look at your relationship with your colleagues and their role in your first year and wrap up our discussion of your first year as a thriving new teacher.

final thoughts
# Becoming a Thriving New Teacher

**A**s a new teacher, you face challenges and opportunities. For many new teachers, the opportunities far outweigh the challenges and teaching becomes a rewarding profession. For others, the day-to-day struggles can add up and weigh them down. These new teachers soon become overwhelmed and may give up or leave the profession. What makes the difference between feeling rewarded and feeling overwhelmed?

The goal of this book has been to identify the six spheres thriving new teachers must address to succeed and which strategies teachers can employ throughout their first year to overcome challenges and feel rewarded instead of overwhelmed. While there are varying opinions about what makes new teachers successful, we have incorporated strategies we have found to be the most useful from our years of experience and our work with many new and experienced teachers.

▶ **Self:** Know who you are, your strengths, and your limitations. Keep in mind your goals as a teacher. This knowledge provides the rudder that will steer you in the right direction—even when you are encountering storms and currents that could take you off track. It will help you stay on course to becoming a thriving new teacher.

▶ **Students and their families:** Making a good first impression and following up to develop a great reputation are critical. People make judgments about others very quickly. The work you do to make a good first impression with your students and their families will get you started on the right foot.

▶ **Classroom management:** Without a well-managed learning environment, students cannot learn and teachers cannot teach. Good classroom management is crucial for your success as a thriving new teacher.

169

▶ **Curriculum management:** As a new teacher, working with the curriculum for the first time can be a daunting experience. As you think about how you'll help students learn while making learning engaging and interesting, you'll see the opportunities to impact students and their success.

▶ **Assessment:** Knowing what to teach is essential but knowing what students have learned is even more important. The formative and summative assessment strategies you use will help you determine the supports students need to learn and then use the content you teach.

▶ **Colleagues:** Throughout the book, we have woven the theme of collaboration and the importance of connecting with your colleagues. No teacher is able to be successful entirely on his or her own. You'll want to make sure that you work to develop the important professional relationships necessary for you and your colleagues to be successful.

As you think about and begin to implement the ideas and strategies we have shared in this book, keep the following points in mind.

▶ It may take time for you to feel comfortable implementing some of the strategies presented here. Everyone learns at a different pace. Give yourself time and be patient with yourself.

▶ Different strategies work better for some teachers than others. Not every strategy presented here will work as well for you as it will for one of your colleagues. Use the strategies that make the most sense for you and your students.

▶ You will develop your own variations of strategies. As you implement the ideas you have learned in this book, feel free to make adaptations and changes. If you personalize what you implement, it will be more meaningful for you.

We hope you have found value in the ideas and strategies we have offered in this book. We wish you well on your journey to becoming a thriving new teacher.

# References & Resources

Assessment for Learning. (n.d.a). *Professional learning: Student self-assessment.* Accessed at www.assessmentforlearning.edu.au/default.asp?id=site_search &query=One+good+question+I+asked+%28or+thought+of%29+today+was+ on July 27, 2015.

Assessment for Learning. (n.d.b). *Strategies to enhance student self-assessment.* Accessed at www.assessmentforlearning.edu.au/professional_learning/ modules/student_self-assessment/student_strategies_enhance.html on July 27, 2015.

Breaux, A. (2002). *101 "Answers" for new teachers and their mentors: Effective teaching tips for daily classroom use.* Larchmont, NY: Eye on Education.

Browner, D., & Spooner, F. (2011). *Teaching students with moderate and severe disabilities.* New York: The Guilford Press.

Common Core State Standards Initiative. (n.d.). *Standards in your state.* Accessed at www.corestandards.org/standards-in-your-state on September 15, 2015.

Covey, S. R. (1989). The seven habits of highly effective people: Powerful lessons in personal change. New York: Simon & Schuster.

Davis, C., & Yang, A. (2005). *Parents and teachers working together.* Turner Falls, MA: Northeast Foundation for Children.

Duek, M. (2014). *Grading smarter, not harder: Assessment strategies that motivate kids and help them learn.* Alexandria, VA: ASCD.

Elden, R. (2013). *See me after class: Advice for teachers by teachers.* Naperville, IL: Sourcebooks.

Eller, J. F. (2004). *Effective group facilitation in education: How to energize meetings and manage difficult groups.* Thousand Oaks, CA: Corwin Press.

Eller, S., & Eller, J. (2006). *Energizing staff meetings.* Thousand Oaks, CA: Corwin Press.

Eller, J. F., & Eller, S. A. (2009). *Creative strategies to transform school culture.* Thousand Oaks, CA: Corwin Press.

Eller, J. F., & Eller, S. A. (2011). *Working with difficult and resistant staff.* Bloomington, IN: Solution Tree Press.

Eller, J. F., & Eller, S. A. (2015). *Score to soar: Moving teachers from evaluation to professional growth*. Bloomington, IN: Solution Tree Press.

Gregory, K., & Cameron, C., & Davies, A. (2011). *Conferencing and reporting* (2nd ed.). Bloomington, IN: Solution Tree Press.

Gregory, G., & Chapman, C. (2013). *Differentiated instructional strategies: One size doesn't fit all*. Thousand Oaks, CA: Corwin Press.

Hattie, J. (2012). *Visible learning for teachers: Maximizing impact on learning*. New York: Routledge.

Jensen, E. (2005). *Teaching with the brain in mind*. Alexandria, VA: ASCD.

Jensen, E. (2016). *Poor students, rich teaching: Mindsets for change*. Bloomington, IN: Solution Tree Press.

Johnson, K., & Cappelloni, N. (2013). *The new teacher's handbook: Flourishing in your first year*. New York: Skyhorse.

Kriegel, O. (2013). *Everything a new elementary school teacher really needs to know (but didn't learn in college)*. Minneapolis: Free Spirit.

Lemov, D. (2010). *Teach like a champion: 49 Techniques that put students on the path to college (K–12)*. San Francisco: Jossey-Bass.

Lipton, L., & Wellman, B. (1999). *Pathways to understanding: Patterns and practices in the learning-focused classroom* (3rd ed.). Guilford, VT: Pathways.

Mandel, S. (2009). *The new teacher toolbox: Proven tips and strategies for a first great year*. Thousand Oaks: Corwin Press.

Marzano, R., & Marzano, J. (2003). *Classroom management that works: Research-based strategies for every teacher*. Alexandria, VA: ASCD.

Marzano, R., & Pickering, D. (2013). *The highly engaged classroom*. Bloomington, IN: Marzano Research.

Mendler, B., & Curwin, R. (2007). *Strategies for successful classroom management: Helping students succeed without losing your dignity or sanity*. Thousand Oaks, CA: Teacher Learning Center/Corwin Press.

Meyers, C., & Jones, T. B. (1993). *Promoting active learning: Strategies for the college classroom*. San Francisco: Jossey-Bass.

Moir, E. (2011, August 17). *Phases of first-year teaching*. Santa Cruz, CA: New Teacher Center. Accessed at www.newteachercenter.org/blog/phases-first-year-teaching on July 27, 2015.

National Education Association. (2015). *National Education Association handbook: 2014–2015*. Accessed at www.nea.org/assets/docs/2015_NEA_Handbook.pdf on July 27, 2015.

National Governors Association Center for Best Practices & Council of Chief State School Officers. (2010). *Common Core State Standards for English language arts and literacy in history/social studies, science, and technical subjects.* Washington, DC: Authors. Accessed at www.corestandards.org/assets/CCSSI_ELA%20Standards.pdf on July 27, 2015.

Parks, J. (2004). *Teacher under construction: Things I wish I'd known! A survival handbook for new middle school teachers.* Lincoln, NE: Weekly Reader Press.

Payne, R. (2013). *A framework for understanding poverty: A cognitive approach.* Highlands, TX: aha! Process.

Schein, E. (1993, Summer). On dialogue, culture, and organizational learning. *Organizational Dynamics*, 22.

Somerville Public Schools. (2015). *The Somerville Public School district is proud to announce that all of our teachers are highly qualified!* Accessed at www.somervillenjk12.org/Page/1644 on July 27, 2015.

Stiggins, R. J., Arter, J. A., Chappuis, J., & Chappuis, S. (2004). *Classroom assessment FOR student learning: Doing it right—Using it well.* Portland, OR: ETS Assessment Training Institute.

Stiggins, R. J., & Chappuis, J. (2006). What a difference a word makes: Assessment FOR learning rather than assessment OF learning helps students succeed. *Journal of Staff Development*, 27(1), 10–14.

Stronge, J., & Xu, X. (2015). *Instructional strategies for effective teaching.* Bloomington, IN: Solution Tree Press.

Thompson, J. (2013). *The first-year teacher's survival guide: Ready-to-use strategies, tools and activities for meeting the challenges of each school day.* San Francisco: John Wiley and Sons.

Tomlinson, C. (2011). *Leading and managing a differentiated classroom.* Alexandria, VA: ASCD.

Whitaker, T., & Flore, T. (2013). *Dealing with difficult parents and parents in difficult situations.* New York: Routledge.

Wiliam, D. (2011). *Embedded formative assessment.* Bloomington, IN: Solution Tree Press.

# Index

### Score to Soar
**By John F. Eller and Sheila A. Eller**
Discover how to guide and enhance the job performance of teachers in your school or district. You'll learn how to evaluate teacher effectiveness, use multiple forms of data for evaluation, and communicate evaluation findings in a way that fosters professional growth.
**BKF625**

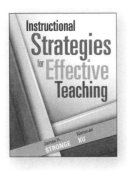

### Working With Difficult & Resistant Staff
**By John F. Eller and Sheila A. Eller**
Identify, confront, and manage all of the difficult and resistant staff you encounter. This book will help school leaders understand how to prevent and address negative staff behaviors to ensure positive school change.
**BKF407**

### Embedded Formative Assessment
**By Dylan Wiliam**
Emphasizing the instructional side of formative assessment, this book explores in depth the use of classroom questioning, learning intentions and success criteria, feedback, collaborative and cooperative learning, and self-regulated learning to engineer effective learning environments for students.
**BKF418**

### Instructional Strategies for Effective Teaching
**By James H. Stronge and Xianxuan Xu**
Discover research-based instructional strategies teachers, coaches, and administrators can use to enhance their everyday practices. Organized around 10 methods of instruction, this user-friendly guide will help you dig deep into classroom discussion, concept mapping, inquiry-based learning, and more.
**BKF641**